W9-BVF-484

Birds of the Eastern Forest: 1

PAINTINGS BY
J. FENWICK LANSDOWNE

TEXT BY
JOHN A. LIVINGSTON

Birds of the Eastern Forest: 1

McCLELLAND AND STEWART

THE CANADIAN PUBLISHERS
*McClelland and Stewart Limited,
25 Hollinger Road, Toronto,
Ontario, Canada*

PRINTED AND BOUND IN GREAT BRITAIN

Contents

Introduction

WHEN we think of the forest, some of us immediately hark back to our childhood to conjure up a picture of a dense, gloomy, silent place fit only for solitary sorcerers and anti-social dragons. Our pioneer ancestors thought of the forest as an implacable enemy to be conquered at all costs, as a matter of survival. A naturalist may think of the forest in terms of the organ-like phrases of a wood thrush, or the distant muffled-drum of a ruffed grouse. Another may recall the springy squelch of sphagnum, or the pungency of skunk cabbage. All these concepts are equally fanciful, of course, because *the* forest as such simply does not exist. There are a number of forest *regions;*each has its own distinctive plant and animal life, and is thus a clearly discernible *biotic* region as well. Some, such as the area under discussion here, have experienced physical change since the time of settlement, and this has greatly influenced their natural history.

Thus, with the exception of mountains, sea-coasts, grasslands, and arctic barrens, which are still clearly identifiable as such and are exactly what their names imply, the regions of Canada are most conveniently catalogued by their forest cover, or by the forest cover they would have if they were in a natural state. Even in an unspoiled, primeval condition, of course, no area is entirely covered by forest. Woodlands are broken and interrupted by meadows and bogs; natural fires caused by lightning open great patches. Ponds, lakes, marshes, and other watercourses are abundant. But in general, and having these qualifications in mind, the landscape is dominated by trees, and the kinds of trees in an area allow us to describe it meaningfully from the naturalist's point of view.

This book's predecessor, *Birds of the Northern Forest* (McClelland and Stewart, Toronto; Houghton Mifflin, Boston; 1966), presented a selection of characteristic birds of the evergreen or boreal region — the great mantle of spruce, fir and larch that covers such a vast portion of Canada. To its north is the treeless tundra. To its south, in the eastern part of the country, is a transition zone of mixed evergreens and deciduous trees. This is the Great Lakes-St. Lawrence Valley region, where the most obvious trees are pine, spruce, yellow birch and maples. Farther east, the Maritime forest region consists mostly of spruces, balsam, yellow birch, maples and pine. The most restricted biotic area in Canada, in a geographic sense, is the Carolinian zone of southern Ontario, which extends along the north shore of Lake Erie and deep into the eastern U.S. This true hardwood forest features several kinds of oaks, with sycamore, tulip-tree, sassafras, hackberry, papaw, hickories and black walnut, none of which occurs elsewhere in Canada. Like the other regions, it has its own special complement of birds, as do the different sorts of habitat within it.

In two volumes, we now look at some of the birds of south-eastern Canada and the eastern United States, where broad-leaved trees and mixed deciduous-evergreen woodlands form the characteristic forest landscape. (This includes the area I grew up in, and live in now, so personal reference will appear in much of what follows.) At one time, great stretches of the east were in pine, most of which has been cut off long since. Under normal conditions, pine is usually succeeded by maple, beech, hemlock, and yellow birch, and in many parts of our area those trees now make up the forest cover. In other places the forest is entirely gone, and fields and urban development have taken its place.

Changes in the face of the land are reflected in changes in animal populations and distributions, including those of birds. From the naturalist's point of view, the Great Lakes-St. Lawrence region is one of the most disturbed areas in North America; alterations in their environment have greatly affected the numbers and ranges of our native birds. During the same period when commercial hunting was draining off such huge numbers of passenger pigeons, the cutting and burning of oak and beech forests removed the habitat of the birds, and they quickly disappeared. The turkey, dependent on the same type of environment, was pushed out of Canada as a wild bird. But as the original forests gradually dwindled and agriculture took their place, new kinds of birds moved in to replace those that had been dispossessed — birds of orchards and "edges," such as eastern bluebirds, robins, and red-headed woodpeckers. Vast areas of cornfields encouraged the spread of the bobwhite and mourning dove.

Then came "clean farming," the general tidying-up of dead trees, old fence-posts and the like, which, together with the introduced European starling, sent several native birds into a precipitous decline. The removal of brushy hedgerows drove out others. Water pollution — by industrial and municipal wastes, and by oil — has reduced feeding, resting and breeding areas for many aquatic birds; marsh drainage and filling have eliminated others. Tourist trespass has crowded out still more.

But, on the credit side, the widespread appearance of mixed second-growth forest has encouraged certain species such as the redstart and the chestnut-sided warbler, which (with white-tailed deer) must be much more numerous today than they were in pioneer times. Human buildings and structures have helped birds such as the eastern phoebe, cliff swallow, chimney swift, and common nighthawk. Even our "scorched-earth" manner of dealing with so much of the landscape has proved of benefit to species such as the killdeer, the horned lark, and the mourning dove. Change is not necessarily good or bad; the outcome depends on the kinds of animals involved, and their requirements.

Not all changes are brought about by man, however. I suppose you could say that the introduction of the Old World elm pestilence was chargeable to ocean transport, but once here, its spread has been entirely natural, through the agency of the elm bark beetles. Although this disease is the horror of arborists and shade-tree conservationists, and has caused savage scarring of the face of the entire region, it has altered some bird distributions for the better. As I pointed out in *Birds of the Northern Forest*, three-toed woodpeckers of both species, normally rather sedentary birds of the boreal zone, have begun to move south each winter in considerable numbers, feeding on the infected elms. There is some evidence (admittedly not a great deal just yet, but we can expect more) that the new abundance of dead-elm nesting sites is encouraging a modest recovery of the red-headed woodpecker and the eastern bluebird.

Even one human lifetime can see remarkable changes in the birdlife of an area. I have talked to men who remembered wild turkey hunting and commercial wildfowling in southern Ontario. What a vastly different country it must have been! Even in my own time, although Cory's least bittern has disappeared from the Toronto lakefront, we have gained the cardinal in great numbers, and to a lesser extent the tufted titmouse and the mockingbird. Pileated woodpeckers have much improved their position over the same period. But birds of prey are diminishing, due to the massive use of chemical pesticides in forestry and agriculture. And there are other kinds of change. Thirty years ago, when Ronald Bremner, Donald Macdonald, Robert Ritchie and I would invite the amusement and scorn of our schoolmates by going *birding* (of all things) at every available opportunity, such an activity was highly suspect. Today, birdwatching is commonplace, and utterly respectable. There are several reasons for this. There is little doubt that an interest in our living environment is one of the measures of a maturing society. At the same time as this interest spread from a small group of experts, Roger Tory Peterson's revolutionary *Field Guide* made it possible for anyone to learn to identify the birds. The new enthusiasts have more time and more money with which to indulge what has become a highly civilized hobby.

Travel has become one of the most popular aspects of recreation and, once he is "hooked," the birder likes to see new species for his list, in new places. He now has a greater opportunity to do so. The hobby of amateur photography is mushrooming; of all subjects, nature is among the most popular – especially birds. Now also, there is every sort of additional "enrichment" for the birdwatcher; an amazing volume of lectures, periodicals, books, prints, sound recordings, films, and broadcasts about birds attract audiences that were undreamed of in my boyhood. Organized bird tours go to such places as Africa, India, Antarctica, and the Galapagos Islands. Almost every city and larger town has its bird club and most of them produce regular journals or other reports. There are international, national, provincial and regional organizations. If you want to learn about birds today, there is no difficulty.

An interesting result of all this is that, of the life sciences, none has profited so greatly from amateur participation as ornithology. People of every level of experience who keep notes of what they see, when, and under what conditions and circumstances, are contributing enormously to the general fund of information. So do those who photograph birds, or band them, or record their voices. Ornithology is the beneficiary.

There is no doubt that the most important result of the explosive growth in birdwatching has been widespread concern – and action – for birds' welfare. Legal protection began only a little over fifty years ago, with the Migratory Bird Treaty (1916) with the United States, and broader, public interest has been even more recent. Today, most birds are protected as a matter of course in civilized countries, and by and large the laws are observed. The loss of bird habitat to unplanned land use has taken longer to gain general appreciation, but there are signs that even that is coming.

This metamorphosis in society's attitude to birds has its parallel in the individual. The man with a casual interest in birds around the garden soon develops a positive desire to keep them there – by feeding, watering, planting for nesting sites, and so on. This is usually followed by at least a germ of curiosity about the names and the ways of the backyard birds, and the quite natural urge to attach a label to some unfamiliar migrant that may turn up in spring or fall. Once that curiosity is satisfied – and further whetted – by the acquisition of a field identification book, the process is near completion. Most people who reach this stage soon appreciate the needs of birds and the environments that sustain them, and actively want to help maintain both. It is a very short and easy step from birds to resources in the broadest sense; birds have given the initial impetus to some of the world's most distinguished conservationists.

As I have pointed out many times in other places, "conservation" is a sorely misunderstood word. There was a time when conservation was virtually synonomous with prohibition; it meant blanket holding-the-line, rigid maintenance of the status quo. But nature is never static; it is dynamic, and changeable. So, somewhat later, conservation came to imply some measure of manipulation or management: the *use* of renewable natural resources with enough forethought to ensure a sustained yield from them. Now, it has become something different still. Conservation (it is time for a new word) involves the whole quality of our lives in an environmental sense. It is human ecology.

Like any bird, man is a living, sensate being, with certain fundamental needs related to all of the other life that surrounds him. We must have trees to provide the oxygen we breathe. We must have soil, water, and a multitude of various organisms to produce our food. But there are human needs above and beyond food, water, air, and shelter, because man is a more complex animal than most. We have needs of the mind and of the spirit. But we cannot satisfy our belly or psyche within a habitat that does not include other living things.

The quality of human life is in peril in a technological, urban age. Conditions in our cities – most especially the stresses resulting from overcrowding – mean that conservation now goes far beyond the special province of the agronomists, the hydrologists, and the biologists. Human ecology must become the concern of architects, urban designers, regional planners, sociologists, anthropologists, artists, medical people, teachers, politicians, and all others who touch upon our daily existence. We are *alive*, and to remain properly so, we must have an environment that includes contact with the natural world from which we sprang, and of which we remain an inseparable part. Conservation is just as much about people as it is about birds.

More than five hundred species of birds have been recorded in Canada, and any selection of species for even one region of the country must be arbitrary. Since it is impossible to be exhaustive in a presentation of this kind, Fenwick Lansdowne and I have chosen what we consider to be a representative sample – but only a sample – of the birds to be found in the mixed and hardwood regions of the east. (Birds recognize no artificial, political boundaries, and all are common in the U.S.) Volume I contains eighteen waterfowl and shorebirds, ten birds of prey, five woodpeckers, five swallows, four flycatchers, and ten others. Volume II will include a selection of the smaller songbirds, from jays to sparrows.

All the birds in this book occur in the east, but a good two-thirds of them are almost country-wide in distribution. Some, such as the rough-winged swallow and the pied-billed grebe, nest over most of the continent. Others – barn owl, common gallinule, common tern, bank swallow – occur in the Old World as well. None is rare; the red-bellied woodpecker, for example, is very limited in range in Canada, but it is common to the south.

The birds are presented in systematic order – grebes to swallows – according to what is generally agreed to be their evolutionary sequence. Perching birds are thought to have evolved more recently than waterbirds such as loons and grebes. (Birds are such perishable, soft-boned creatures, however, that the fossil record of ornithology is regrettably slim.) The order and the nomenclature are those of the *1957 Check-list of North American Birds* published by the American Ornithologists' Union. Length and (where necessary) wingspread for each species appear in a foot-note.

These are portraits of individual birds that once were living, painted from skins lent to Fenwick Lansdowne by museums. Since both the date and place of capture will be of interest to some readers, these are provided in an appendix. The geographic origin of some skins may not coincide with the stated area of this book, but that is no more than a reflection of the widespread distribution of some species.

In many species of birds, the sexes are distinctly different in pattern and colour. In others, they are to all intents and purposes identical. In still others, the sexes are distinguishable in the field, but there is sufficient similarity between the two that identification of the species is not in doubt. This has guided the artist throughout. For example, although male and female black ducks do not have precisely the same colouring, it was not considered necessary to illustrate them both. The "family" resemblance is enough.

The text is not arranged formally under standard sub-headings for each species (description, field marks, distribution, habits, nest, eggs, etc.). This information is available from a great many sources in a wide and rich literature. W. Earl Godfrey's *The Birds of Canada* (National Museum of Canada, 1966) is recommended for reference purposes. A limited bibliography suggests additional reading and source material. Since there is nothing more tedious in a popular book than a constant barrage of formal attributions and foot-notes, these have been dispensed with. But my indebtedness to the literature is quite evident throughout; every naturalist is as dependent on his library as a bird is on its feeding territory.

The purpose of the following text is obviously not to present a definitive treatment of eastern birds. It is, however, an attempt to provide a number of selected glimpses into a world that is not ours, but one that we can freely enter anywhere, any time. The aim has been to illuminate to some extent the *fact* of birds in their beauty and diversity, and to illustrate some of the simple pleasures and more lasting intellectual challenges that are so readily available to us in their world. But more than that, I have occasionally called attention to the plight of some troubled species. The birds are important to Fenwick Lansdowne and me, and a plea for their preservation is implicit throughout.

The more you travel and the more intensively you pursue a preoccupation, the more people there are to whom you become indebted. But I am always most conscious of those whose roots are in common with mine and whose lives and interests are interwoven with my own. Especially valued, over many years in the Great Lakes region, has been the inspiration and warm companionship provided by James L. Baillie, H. J. M. Barnett, Lucius F. Barnett, Fred Bodsworth, William H. Carrick, John Crosby, William W. H. Gunn, Eric Nasmith, Donald Pace, Roger Tory Peterson, Jack Satterly, Richard M. Saunders, T. M. Shortt, William W. Smith, Earl V. Stark, Robert W. Trowern, and my wife, Peggy, none of whom bears any responsibility for errors of commission or omission between these covers, but all of whom are indelibly identified with unforgettable moments and deeply satisfying years among the birds. Neither are any textual inadequacies chargeable to those who contributed most, in a variety of ways, to the existence of this volume: William R. Banting, Sylvia L. Danter, M. F. Feheley, Leslie Hannon, John G. McClelland, and Anne Tait.

This was written with my father's memory ever in mind. He knew nothing about birds, but he knew a lot about encouragement.

John A. Livingston

Indispensable to any painter of birds is access to a wide selection of skins; for years my source has been the Royal Ontario Museum, and about half the following paintings were done from birds in its collection. James L. Baillie, of the Department of Birds, once again has given much time and attention to choosing the best examples.

With two exceptions, the remaining skins used were lent by the kindness of Dr. S. Dillon Ripley, Secretary of the Smithsonian Institution, who, when my other arrangements became impractical, freely made available the collection of the United States National Museum. Gorman M. Bond, Research Assistant to Dr. Ripley, kindly undertook the selecting and shipping of the birds.

The figures of the Virginia rail and the female pileated woodpecker were taken from skins in the possession of the Provincial Museum of British Columbia, for the use of which I thank Dr. G. Clifford Carl.

I owe a particular debt of gratitude to another person, Peter Cook, on whose good taste and advice I have frequently relied. In other, technical, ways, not readily apparent to the viewer of these paintings, his help has been considerable.

J. Fenwick Lansdowne

plate 1 — the sketch

PIED-BILLED GREBE

Podilymbus podiceps

plate 1   PIED-BILLED GREBE *Podilymbus podiceps*

IN the declining years of the 19th century and the first decade or so of this, the commercial trade in bird feathers and skins was still in full swing. Major victims of the professional hunters were egrets and herons, roseate spoonbills, trumpeter swans—and grebes. It is difficult, perhaps, to see now just what contribution a grebe could possibly make to the fashion salons of the time, but apparently their breasts were in demand by milliners—presumably for the softness and density of the feathering. All that ended, of course, with the Migratory Bird Treaty of 1916; since then, apart from a widespread habitat loss, grebes have led a reasonably secure existence.

Unnatural mass mortality by commercial hunting and marsh drainage is one thing; natural hazards are another. I well remember walking around Grenadier Pond in Toronto one very cold winter day. The pond was frozen except, strangely enough, for one very small pool, no more than two feet in diameter. As I watched it curiously, up in the middle popped a pied-billed grebe. Perhaps the bird's activity had helped to keep the hole open, but its chance of survival seemed slim as it could not become airborne. Like a loon, the grebe is so well adapted for swimming that it has lost much of its aerial prowess. Once in the air it is safe enough, but its wings are short, and it needs a rather long stretch of water for takeoff.

But, in nature, everything seems to even up. If grebes have limitations for flight, they are marvellously adapted to the water. Notice especially this bird's grotesque feet. The toes of loons, ducks, and geese have webs between them; those of grebes are not webbed, but they have become extraordinarily flat. Each toe has, in fact, become a finlike lobe. In motion, the foot as a whole acts like a frogman's flipper: it widens to its fullest extent on the powerful thrusting stroke, and slims down on the return stroke to lower water resistance. Underwater, the grebe uses only its feet for propulsion, and is quite speedy enough to dine well on small fishes, crustaceans, and aquatic insects.

In the nesting season, this is the shyest of our grebes. If its pond is not large enough to allow a good open sheet of water, it will nearly always hide from an observer, behind some clump or sprig of vegetation. If you approach, it will without any apparent effort gradually submerge until only its head is showing. Move even closer, and with an abrupt little "duck-dive" it will somersault beneath the surface and dart away underwater. Sometimes you will have a difficult time finding it when it surfaces; often you will not see it again. This performance gave rise to one of the bird's nicknames, "helldiver," because it appeared to go straight down and never return. Some grebes can dive to depths of twenty-three metres.

Most of our grebes are sociable, gregarious animals that breed in colonies. The pied-bill is the exception. In winter you will see numbers on southern and sub-tropical ponds, living together amicably enough, and they flock on their northward migration, but once they arrive on their breeding grounds they tend to become very jealous of their nesting territories. The nest is built on floating marsh vegetation. The "loudly" striped young birds commonly ride on the parents' backs, both on the surface and below.

This species occurs throughout our hemisphere. In Canada it breeds on fresh water, chiefly east of the Rockies, with a rather small pocket in southern British Columbia. The best identification mark is the peculiar, chickenlike bill.

Length 13 inches. Wingspread 2 feet.   Female, Favourable Lake Mine, Ontario, June 13.
Omemee, Ontario, June 1.

plate 2 – the sketch

GREAT BLUE HERON
Ardea herodias

plate 2 GREAT BLUE HERON *Ardea herodias*

RAKING and lurching to a mid-air stall, wide, deeply-cambered wings beating frantically, long stick-like legs awkwardly flailing for support, a great blue heron in the process of landing is anything but graceful. But there is a reason for this cumbersome attempt at helicoptering. The heron's legs are its livelihood, and if one should be damaged in alighting in a tall tree, the consequences could be serious. It may look amusing to us, but it is a life-or-death matter for the heron.

This is our largest heron, a good four feet tall. In rural parts of the country it is often called "crane," but the two families are not allied. Herons are characterized by long, strong, tapered beaks mounted on even longer, highly flexible necks. They usually fly with their heads tucked back on their shoulder; cranes keep their necks outstretched. The great blue is an expert still-fisherman; it will stand on a bank or in shallow water without a single movement for agonizing periods of time, never flinching. Then, ever so slowly, the neck is gradually extended, often at an odd angle, bringing the formidable beak into striking position. Almost imperceptibly, the great head is lowered. Suddenly, with a movement your eye can scarcely follow, a horny javelin flashes beneath the surface, to reappear momentarily with a fish, a frog, or some other aquatic animal. (Insects, mice, small birds and other items are also common in the great blue's diet.) The prey is swallowed with more or less ease, depending on its size; the heron delicately takes a sip or two of water, and settles down again to its vigil.

This is the most numerous of its family in Canada. It breeds on the west coast, and east of the Rockies in a fairly shallow band to the Maritimes, its range coinciding with the most heavily settled portions of the country. It has a wide range of habitats—rivers, lakeshores, marshes, mudflats, ponds, streams— watery places of all kinds, whether fresh or salt. All it needs is a supply of aquatic prey. But even though its requirements are elastic in this respect, the great blue heron is rigidly bound to its special need of mature trees for nesting purposes, in appropriate seclusion. Privacy is becoming one of the rarest commodities of our time, and the herons are beginning to pay the price. Colonies are fewer and fewer.

This is a large, relatively slow-moving bird that has always been a fetching target for the trigger-happy. It is protected by law, but statutory guardianship is of limited value off the beaten track. Even quite innocent and well-meaning intrusion into its colonies by photographers and others can cause the birds to desert their nests.

Most Canadian great blue herons are migratory, but a few manage to survive the winter. When they return in spring, the male takes up a territory around last year's nest. Although the birds are highly competitive about precise breeding sites within their colony, and defend the immediate vicinity of the nest, they are more communal in their feeding habits. Some may own preferred fishing areas in which they discourage other great blue herons, but this is more likely in the non-breeding season. It is quite unusual to find a pair of these herons nesting solitarily; at that time they prefer the company of their own kind. In colonies which include other species of herons, which is frequently the case, the great blues will usually be found in the tallest trees.

The usual clutch of eggs is four. New nestlings in their fuzzy down are not easily described; perhaps a bottle-brush provides the most apt simile.

Length 46 inches. Wingspread 5¹/₂-6 feet.   Male, Willowdale, Ontario, April 4.

plate 3 — the sketch

GREEN HERON

Butorides virescens

plate 3

GREEN HERON *Butorides virescens*

CANADA's next-to-smallest heron is credited with one of the more remarkable accomplishments in the bird world. It is known to have attracted prey by offering bait. Harvey B. Lovell, of the University of Louisville, was watching a green heron fishing in Florida. He threw the bird a piece of bread which it picked up and placed in the water, allowing it to slowly float away. When it drifted almost out of reach, the heron recovered it and placed it close by again. Soon the bird caught a fish which had come to nibble on the bread. Lovell threw it another piece – this time a good distance back on the land. The bird quickly retrieved it and placed it in the water as bait. When some coots came by, the heron gathered in his bait and drove them away, and then placed it back in the water when they had passed.

In his account in *The Wilson Bulletin,* Lovell says: "A clear indication that the green heron knew what he was doing was furnished by the following incident. While he was standing by some floating bread, several small fish broke the surface of the water several feet to his left. The heron immediately became excited, picked up his bread and moved it to almost the exact spot where the fish had appeared." Here you have a member of a family that is not exactly renowned for sagacity evidently capable of learning something quite sophisticated. Was this an example of the abstract recognition of cause and effect, or was it only a fortunate accident? It is impossible to dismiss it as the latter.

The green heron's normal fishing technique, though less dramatic, is by no means pedestrian. It usually perches on small branches close to the water and deftly snatches up small prey as it comes along. Occasionally it will jump in – or even plunge, kingfisher-fashion. This diving can be important when the need arises. Alexander Sprunt IV, of the National Audubon Society, once saw a green heron dive into the water to avoid a hawk that was in swift pursuit.

When it is alarmed, the green heron flicks its tail nervously and will often erect a shaggy, ragged crest. If approached, it will "freeze" in one of a variety of unlikely postures, hoping that protective coloration and absolute immobility will allow it to remain unnoticed. If pressed too closely, it will burst into the air, legs dangling, crest erect, neck extended at a crazy angle, voicing a hoarse *quow!* as it goes. In more leisurely flight it looks blackish, much like a crow, but with shorter wings and a longer bill. For a heron, this one is surprisingly manoeuvrable in the air, and makes its way among tangles and thickets with ease. Its aerobatics are especially interesting in courtship flight, when both sexes clap their wings sharply beneath their bodies.

Unlike most herons, this species is not particularly sociable. It is usually a solitary nester, although limited groups are found occasionally. Outside the breeding season, any gregariousness that may have been achieved in a colony is promptly lost. This bird is every bit the self-sufficient individual – a character implicit in Fenwick Lansdowne's portrait.

Green herons are scattered widely over this hemisphere, but in Canada they breed only in southern Ontario, extreme southern Quebec and New Brunswick. Like all our herons, they are forced to be migratory.

Length 18 inches. Wingspread 2 feet.   Female, Long Point, Norfolk Co., Ontario, May 4.

plate 4 — the sketch

BLACK-CROWNED NIGHT HERON

Nycticorax nycticorax

plate 4 BLACK-CROWNED NIGHT HERON *Nycticorax nycticorax*

THE several members of the heron tribe in Canada are all worthy of our attention, but this one has a special appeal. The others are mostly daytime feeders, and more or less conspicuous. The night heron's unusual appearance, its reclusive nature by day and its mysterious wanderings at night combine with its strange guttural voice to give it a most intriguing personality.

Most herons are more or less social, at least at times, but this one is especially gregarious. It roosts and nests in crowded colonies, in somewhat fetid conditions, although individuals will stake out and maintain their own favourite fishing grounds. The birds rest motionless and silent in the dense cover of trees during the day, waiting until dusk to venture forth for their night-long hunting. It is at late twilight that you will most enjoy watching them, as their sturdy, thickset bodies move on broad wings in silhouette, with an occasional deep-throated *quock!* to announce their passing. They work in shallow water, chiefly on coarse fish, crayfish, frogs and various insects, but they will turn to small mammals such as mice and voles if the opportunity arises. Usually they concentrate on still-fishing, but they will sometimes stalk their prey, and they are able to do some swimming. Food items are usually modest in size, but I have seen one bird with an immense catfish which took him more than an hour to swallow.

This unusually interesting species has the distinction of having been involved in what would seem to be the very first scientific experiments in bird banding in America. In 1902, P. Bartsch made up some special bands which he put on the legs of black-crowned night herons taken in colonies near Washington, D.C. The bands carried serial numbers, the year of the experiment, and the instruction to return them to the Smithsonian Institution. He banded twenty-three birds, of which one was recovered not far away in Maryland. Bartsch carried on in subsequent years, and one of his birds turned up in Cuba, another in Toronto. Thus a research activity was launched that has had immeasurable influence on our knowledge of the seasonal movements of birds, their routes, their longevity, and many other kinds of information that could be gathered in no other way.

Few herons are so compatible with human settlement as the black-crowned night heron. Although it is no more immune to overt disturbance than any other heron, it seems able to tolerate close contact with man, persisting to this day within the borders of large cities. Here, however, it runs the risk of contamination through its food by the various and virulent effluents of the affluent society. Insecticidal residues and other toxic substances in the water, together with industrial and municipal wastes, are making its fishing grounds ever less attractive and productive.

Nesting colonies are characteristically jammed, active, and noisy. Courting and mated birds seem to recognize each other by their head plumes alone, not by coloration. Vigorous fights over territorial invasion sometimes develop between neighbours; contesting birds advance upon each other in a threatening low crouch from which they attempt to seize the opponent's bill, head, or wing. This is accompanied by a multitude of indescribable noises, most of them throaty and squawking. The nest is built of coarse sticks and twigs, with a finer lining. Little if any attempt is made at sanitation; the person of delicate sensitivity should keep his distance from a black-crowned night heron colony.

This species is readily identified by its stocky build, its rather short and heavy bill, and its generally grey colour. Young birds are speckled brown. In flight, night herons look especially chunky and neckless. This is virtually a cosmopolitan bird, and it nests in almost every imaginable wooded situation, but its colonies in Canada are spotty. Major centres are the central and southeastern prairies, the lower Great Lakes and the St. Lawrence valley. Farther south, you find the related and somewhat similar yellow-crowned night heron, but it rarely ventures as far north as Canada.

Length 25 inches. Wingspread 3³/₄ feet.   Male, Islington, York Co., Ontario, Sept. 16.

plate 5 — the sketch

LEAST BITTERN
Ixobrychus exilis

plate 5 LEAST BITTERN *Ixobrychus exilis*

Our most secretive and tiniest heron, no bigger than a dove, is also by far the most difficult to find and observe. It is the least likely to fly, preferring to run and creep through the marsh cattails. It seems nowhere common, but it is probably a good deal more numerous than most of us can prove by personal experience. Once found, however, this little bird is worth all your patience and, if you keep perfectly still, sometimes you may be able to watch it for extended periods.

There is much less difficulty in hearing one. The bird has a very wide, varied vocabulary. One of the more recognizable notes is a dovelike *coo* which it makes in springtime. In addition, there are other calls which, if you are not careful, you might credit to some of the least bittern's neighbours – gallinules or coots, pied-billed grebes, or even frogs.

This bird behaves much more like a rail than a heron, stalking about among dense sedges, grasses, and bulrushes, always staying very close to the ground. If you disturb it, it will vanish in a trice – on foot. Sometimes, if you are lucky, it will jump into the air and fly weakly for a short distance, revealing yellowish-buff patches on warm chestnut wings.

There is a rare colour phase of the least bittern, in which the pale areas are replaced by reddish chestnut. At one time this was thought to be a distinct species, and it went by the name of Cory's least bittern (*Ixobrychus neoxena*). This was one of the more important birds of my boyhood, as its world centre of abundance happened to be in the marshes around Ashbridge's Bay in Toronto. I never saw one alive, but there was always the possibility, in those magic times when something new happened every day, that just one more early-morning visit to the marshes would pay off.

There *was* one, however, with which I had close association. This was a mounted Cory's – old and badly eroded – that teetered in an ancient glass case in the high school I attended. This was a significant bird, and it deserved more appropriate quarters; in the course of time James Baillie, of the Royal Ontario Museum, persuaded my biology teacher to donate it to the R.O.M.'s distinguished collection. Regrettably, our headmaster learned of the arrangement and immediately vetoed it. After all these years, I have no idea where that rare specimen eventually came to rest; perhaps it has served to inspire subsequent generations of schoolboys.

That "Cory's" least bittern has been down-graded from a full species to a colour phase is, however, no indication of its diminishing importance. Colour phases and their role in evolution are of great interest; they are well known in animals such as screech owls and grey squirrels. The mysterious chestnut bird should still be watched for, wherever there are least bitterns. Some may remain at Lake Okeechobee, Florida, or in the Long Point marshes of Lake Erie. But it will not be seen again at Ashbridge's Bay, which has long since become the site of a sewage filtration plant.

Although this bird is habitually terrestrial, it is an agile climber, and nearly always builds its nest above ground level. The nest is a structure of very little substance, but it is strong enough to hold the four or five greenish-white eggs which both parents incubate. This is not a colonial heron; nests are usually solitary. Near the nest, the birds are more likely to attempt to conceal themselves by "freezing" than by running or flying. It has been reported that the birds have such faith in their unmoving posture that they can be approached and picked up in the hand. Even downy young will freeze; this is clearly an innate behaviour pattern that they have not had time to learn.

Least bitterns are completely dependent on the availability of fresh-water marshes. As wetlands are being drained and filled everywhere, especially in the more southern parts of the country, the future of the bird seems to be limited to whatever areas of natural habitat we eventually see fit to leave it. It lives chiefly in southern Ontario (where marshes are disappearing fastest), with small outposts in southern Manitoba and southern New Brunswick.

Length 13 inches. Wingspread 1¹/₂ feet.   Male, Hamilton, Ontario, June 1.

plate 6 — the sketch

AMERICAN BITTERN

Botaurus lentiginosus

plate 6 AMERICAN BITTERN *Botaurus lentiginosus*

THE bittern never perches in trees. It is almost always on the ground, and very rarely leaves the cover of dense marsh vegetation. It is most noteworthy for its dedicated practice of the art of self-concealment by "freezing." The bird is marked and coloured astonishingly like the dead reeds and cattails of its surroundings, and when it chooses to strike a motionless posture it can be almost impossible to see. It usually takes a rigid stance with its bill held stiffly in the air, its feathers tightly compressed as though in an attempt to become a tuft of grass. It remains immobile, staring at you glassily over its bill; some observers have seen it sway perceptibly, as though in rhythm with the movement of the vegetation. If you move around it slowly, it will also move, in order to keep facing you. Lester Snyder and Shelley Logier, of the Royal Ontario Museum, once repeatedly circled a bittern in this way, to a point where the bird got itself so turned and twisted around that it ended careened on its side and partially under water! Such is the bittern's unshakable faith in camouflage.

The big "thunder-pumper" or "stake-driver" has a wide range in Canada, from central British Columbia and Great Slave Lake to James Bay and Newfoundland, southward wherever there are suitable wet fields, bogs, and marshes. The nicknames derive from the bird's voice. Its deep, booming call, especially in spring, consists of three or four syllables, preceded (at close range) by sharp clicks of the bill. The sound is delivered by means of the bird swallowing air; it consists simply of well-regulated "burps." It carries well, although at a distance its low frequency and muffled quality sometimes make the source difficult to pinpoint.

This is another solitary-nesting heron. Two or more nests close together have been thought to be evidence of polygamy rather than of social nesting. Females appear to look after the young by themselves. The nest is a sort of platform made of marsh vegetation a mere four or five inches above the level of the water. If you approach the nest and the freezing posture doesn't work, the bittern explodes out of the vegetation in front of you, flaps hurriedly on wide, brown wings to another part of the marsh, and heavily plops in again.

The long, strong bill is an efficient instrument for snatching up marsh animals such as mice, small birds, fishes, crayfish and frogs. It can also be a weapon of defence. Robie W. Tufts has a splendid account of this in *The Birds of Nova Scotia*. "On one occasion I banded and released a juvenile in a field near a cattail swamp where cattle were pastured. Drawn by curiosity, a large steer that had been watching the operation at fairly close quarters drew near with head lowered, sniffing audibly, as though to investigate. Meanwhile, the bird, instead of beating a hasty retreat to cover, as it could well have done, stood its ground, and with head drawn in close to its body, glared menacingly at the steer. Finally, and with a suggestion of timidity, the steer's nose came within inches of the poised bird. Suddenly the sharp beak shot out and upward, stabbing the animal viciously on the tender part of the nostril; whereupon, with a loud snort, the steer turned and went galloping across the field. The bird, after gaining its composure, strode off slowly in a dignified manner and soon disappeared."

There are bitterns of the genus *Botaurus* on four continents; they are very similar, and some authorities consider them all one species. Our bird seems to be an inveterate wanderer on migration; there are more than forty records of its occurrence in the United Kingdom.

Length 27 inches. Wingspread 3¹/₄ feet. *Male, C. Henrietta Maria, Kenora Dist., Ontario, July 5.*

plate 7 – the sketch

BLACK DUCK
Anas rubripes

plate 7   BLACK DUCK *Anas rubripes*

THIS sturdy, splendid duck is the second most important migratory waterfowl in Canada; it is to the east what the mallard is to the west. Swift, sagacious, implacably wild, it is one of the hardiest of its family. Cold weather does not bother the big "black mallard," as New Englanders call it. It frequently arrives for spring nesting while ice still covers many of its ponds and streams, and egg-laying and even incubation may be under way before the snow disappears.

Ducks are jealous of their nesting territories, and wild aerial chases are frequent sights in late April. Sometimes these pursuits degenerate into common fights, with drakes driving off other drakes and even pursuing other pairs. For nesting, the birds like good cover, usually the shelter of low bushes or tall grass. The female chooses the site and makes a shallow cup out of available materials. The first egg is laid in about nine or ten days, and the full clutch of about nine eggs is complete ten days later. Now, incubation begins, and the drake leaves the area to join other new bachelors on a nearby pond.

Ducklings become "imprinted" on the first moving thing they see and hear, soon after hatching. Generally this object is their mother, and the bond between parent and young keeps the brood together, and thus safer, than if each individual were wandering about on its own. That is why bunches of small ducklings always walk and swim in such close-knit, tight formation behind the duck. The young waste no time in learning to fend for themselves, and almost immediately begin a diligent search for small invertebrates, and other food. Animal protein is essential to strong early growth. The birds will fly when they are eight or nine weeks old. As soon as they are effectively airborne, they part company with their mothers, gathering in large groups.

In July and August the black ducks begin to move from small ponds to larger lakes and marshes, and from there they push on to the Atlantic shore; gradually great migrant and wintering flocks build up along the coast. Courtship and pair formation against the following spring have taken place by this time (ducks, noted for their concupiscence, make it a short off-season), and pairs remain together over the winter. Much wishful-thinking anthropomorphic rubbish has been promulgated about birds possessed of such fidelity that they mate for life and remain celibate after the disappearance of one of the pair, but a few facts help maintain the attractive notion. There are at least two recorded instances in which a black duck, whose partner was shot by gunners, refused to leave its mate.

The black duck is a dabbler, that is, it feeds at the surface of a pond by immersing its head in the water and tipping its bottom into the air. This group also includes mallards, pintail, wigeon, shovelers, and the various teal. They are characterized by a broad, spatulate bill which is equipped with sieves along its sides, making it possible for the bird to sift and strain water for tiny bits of food. These ducks are so closely related that they frequently hybridize: especially blacks, mallards, and pintail.

On the Atlantic coast during winter the black ducks eat snails, periwinkles, mussels and other shellfish. When they arrive on the fresh-water breeding grounds in our latitudes, they switch their diet to the seeds of sedges, rushes, and such plants. They are found in summer south from Ungava and eastern Manitoba, with occasional nesting in Saskatchewan and Alberta. Unlike the cosmopolitan mallard, this species is strictly North American. Many shooters claim it is the most challenging game waterfowl in the world.

Length 23 inches. Wingspread 3 feet.   Male, Nettichi River, James Bay, Ontario, July 19.

plate 8 – the sketch

WOOD DUCK

Aix sponsa

plate 8

WOOD DUCK *Aix sponsa*

*F*ENWICK Lansdowne's brilliant portrait spares me the task of even attempting to describe the male wood duck – surely the most gorgeous waterfowl in the world. The flamboyance of the drake is approached only by the male mandarin duck of east Asia. Although the latter is quite dissimilar in colour and pattern, the females of the two are nearly indistinguishable. They are both perching ducks, which nest in trees.

Audubon knew this bird as the "summer duck," and his Romantic prose outdoes even *his* luxuriant style when he describes it. On the earthbound, factual side he stated that the female bird transports the downy ducklings in her bill from the nesting hole to the water. There seems little evidence of this. Apparently the small birds just tumble out and fall lightly to the ground beneath. Sharp little claws on their toes no doubt enable them to clamber out of the nesting hollow in the first place.

The hole itself is sometimes the former home of a large woodpecker, such as a pileated, or even a flicker. Wood ducks seem to be able to compress themselves remarkably to enter openings that would seem to be far too small for them. Most often, however, the nest is in a natural cavity in a tree, up to fifty feet from the ground. It does not need to be over the water or even very near it; the birds are perfectly prepared to make the chicks undertake a substantial overland hike to their first swim.

Wood ducks are readily attracted to artificial nesting sites. One of the easiest to construct is simply an old nail keg with an entrance hole about four inches in diameter, set on a pole over the water. Wood chips or sawdust should be placed inside, and a hole cut in the bottom for drainage. Putting it over the water discourages predators of various kinds.

In Illinois, students conducted an investigation of 820 unsuccessful nestings of wood ducks over a seventeen-year period. They discovered that the losses were chargeable 51% of the time to fox squirrels, 37% raccoons, 10% snakes, and 2% opossums. In Canada, raccoons are the most common offenders. A nesting box on a pole in the water is the best defence. But predation is the natural thing, and we should not concern ourselves about it unduly. The economy of nature simply could not cope with the survival of a dozen new wood ducks each year from every mated pair.

At one time this bird was very abundant in eastern North America. But it is a somewhat tame and unwary creature, and gunners brought such pressure to bear that it soon became extremely difficult to see a wood duck anywhere. It was placed on the protected list for a time, and began to recoup somewhat. It is by no means out of the woods yet, however, and the irony of the situation is that if it were permitted to, it could probably become one of our most common and most familiar water birds.

Richard Pough wrote in 1951: "Unfortunately, the two millions or so of our citizens who hunt ducks have not been willing to exempt from hunting even this one rather small species so that the 150 million of us who do not hunt can have it around in abundance where we can enjoy its beauty." Nothing much has changed in the meantime, save the numbers of people. In 1967, Ontario shooters were still permitted to kill four wood ducks per day, with a possession limit of eight, inconceivable though it may seem to many of us that anyone could wittingly destroy one.

In Canada the wood duck occurs in southern B.C., central Saskatchewan, south-central Manitoba, southern Ontario, extreme southern Quebec, and, in a limited way, in the Maritimes.

Length 18 inches. Wingspread 2¹/₄ feet.   Male, Mud Lake, Scott Tp., Ontario Co., Ontario, October 6.
Female, Ashbridges Bay, Toronto, Ontario, October 16.

plate 9 — the sketch

TURKEY VULTURE

Cathartes aura

plate 9

TURKEY VULTURE *Cathartes aura*

THE name of the bird clearly has nothing whatever to do with its family relationships; "turkey" is merely for the bare red head of the adult. This is the only vulture that occurs in Canada on a regular basis; the black vulture of the south turns up only on very rare occasions. Happily, this great bird seems to be extending its range in our country; it has moved into all the provinces from Ontario westward.

The vulture shows conspicuous adaptations for its way of life. The head is not feathered, for sanitary reasons; feeding on carrion can be a messy job. The feet are small and relatively weak for a bird of this proportion, for, as Roger Tory Peterson has aptly put it, "its prey cannot escape." It finds its food by quartering the landscape in graceful, effortless, soaring flight, which is made possible by especially well-developed tendons and ligaments in the wings. A notable reduction in breast muscles (they aren't needed for soaring) is evident in the bird's heavy, ponderous flapping as it leaves the ground. This species shows a conspicuous dihedral in soaring flight, and tends to rock gently from side to side as it takes advantage of thermal columns and updrafts from cliffsides and other sources.

It has long been disputed whether vultures find their food by eyesight or by a highly developed sense of smell. As long ago as the 1830s, John James Audubon was busy conducting experiments (exposing one carcass, covering another) which indicated to his satisfaction that the vulture uses only its eyes. Later experiments did not seem to be conclusive, with results going both ways. The controversy continues to this day. In areas where vultures are more common, however, such as tropical Africa, eyesight would *seem* to be the key.

Vultures are usually in attendance within minutes of a big cat's daytime kill, often before the victim is dead. They get their clue by seeing the descent of other vultures. Rare is the carcass that remains uneaten long enough for putrefaction to provide any evidence of its presence. Possibly, sensory development varies between species of vultures, or groups of species.

The turkey vulture builds no formal nest. It lays its two eggs directly on the ground in a hillside cave or crevice, under a stump or hollow log, or on a cliff ledge. Young birds are in the "nest" for at least two months before they take to the air. Delicacy prevents my describing the odoriferous feeding of the chicks at this stage; that is best left to one's imagination. As in all large birds, the young spend much time in wing-exercising as they grow larger, with strenuous flapping, and stretching. An interesting sidelight on this is the report that a young vulture kept in a cage until three months of age, in such close confinement that it could not exercise its wings, was unable to fly when released.

Although their food habits are repugnant to people, vultures obviously play a very important role in the economy of nature, especially in warmer parts of the world. Without the activities of this "sanitation squad," equatorial regions would be much less pleasant places than they are. In many areas they cluster in streets and backyards, as tolerant of human approach as domestic pigeons. There are vultures of various kinds, including the condors, throughout our hemisphere; the closest relative of our species is the very similar yellow-headed vulture of Central and South America. Old World vultures, which are not related to our birds, inhabit southern Europe, Africa, and Asia.

Length 29 inches. Wingspread 5³/₄-6 feet. Female, Salmon R. near Beaver L., Lennox and Addington Cos., Ontario, November 20.

plate 10 – the sketch

SHARP-SHINNED HAWK

Accipiter striatus

plate 10   SHARP-SHINNED HAWK *Accipiter striatus*

Of our three accipiters, the bird-eating true hawks, this is the smallest. It is no larger than a mourning dove, and thus the birds it eats are generally those of the size of sparrows or warblers, although it will not hesitate to attack larger targets upon occasion. It does not restrict itself to birds, however, and will take small mammals and large insects from time to time.

In all hawks, the females are perceptibly larger than the males. This can result in some confusion between this species and the quite similar Cooper's hawk. A large female sharp-shin may be almost the same size as a small male Cooper's, in which case you can differentiate between them by the shape of the tip of the tail, which is square or notched in the sharp-shin, rounded in the Cooper's.

As hunters, these birds are the last word in cool efficiency. They are very fast, very strong, and highly manoeuvrable, making their swift and silent way through dense woodlands and tangled shrubbery with no apparent effort – places that other birds of prey would never attempt. The typical accipiter flight pattern consists of several quick flaps of the wings followed by a short sail, then more flapping, then sail again. This characteristic locomotion, together with their shortish, rounded wings and long tails, separates the accipiters from all other birds of prey.

As a group, these hawks have been among the most violently persecuted of our birds. All birds of prey are disliked by some people, but the accipiters, because of their food habits, have long been subject to massive, senseless attack. Sharp-shinned hawks are spectacular migrants, and on their autumnal flights southward they are relatively easy prey to those who would destroy them. Formerly, before enlightened legislation prevented it, there used to be great hawk shoots at key migration points such as

Cape May, New Jersey. In *Birds Over America*, Roger Tory Peterson tells of having seen, in 1935, some 800 sharp-shins attempt to cross the firing lines. "Each time a 'sharpy' sailed over the treetops it was met by a pattern of lead. Some folded up silently; others, with head wounds, flopped to the ground, chattering shrilly. By noon 254 birds lay on the pavement." But those were the old days, and such organized kills are things of the past. Although uninformed or indifferent individual hunters still take their toll today, it is much less severe.

One of the finest places to watch the fall migration of sharp-shinned hawks is Point Pelee National Park, in extreme south-western Ontario. Here, great flights of birds proceeding south-westerly along the north shore of Lake Erie are funnelled down the point and out across the end of the lake. I have counted more than 1,000 sharp-shins there in a single day. One morning, when there was an especially heavy flight of songbirds *and* hawks at the tip of the peninsula, one sharp-shin was in such relentless pursuit of a yellow warbler as it shot round a red cedar that it could not change course in time to avoid running straight into James Baillie, who was standing beside me. But accipiters are rarely unable to control their movements; they are among the most agile of predatory birds.

This is essentially a wilderness species, inhabiting the forest country from coast to coast. It does not like human company, and usually avoids settled areas. Occasionally one will take up residence near a winter bird-feeding station, which can pose a delicate question of policy. But we must always remember that predation is an essential factor in the economics of nature, and that the culling of surpluses is inescapable and necessary. There are a lot more chickadees and juncos than there are sharp-shinned hawks.

Length 12 inches. Wingspread 2 feet.   Female, Kingsville, Essex Co., Ontario, September 18.

plate 11 — the sketch

RED-SHOULDERED HAWK

Buteo lineatus

plate 11   RED-SHOULDERED HAWK *Buteo lineatus*

THE word "hawk" for members of the genus *Buteo* is a misnomer. The true hawks are the sharp-shin, the Cooper's, and the goshawk — the bird-eaters. The red-shoulder and its relatives are soarers that catch their prey by dropping on it from above, not by pursuit. It follows that they kill very few birds, simply because most buteos are not sufficiently nimble to catch them. So they eat mostly small mammals, reptiles and amphibians, and large insects. They will also eat crustaceans, and I have seen a red-shouldered hawk catch an unwary panfish by plopping into the water on top of it from a low overhanging branch.

This is a comparatively inactive creature for a bird of prey, and (especially in the south) an unsuspicious one. It spends most of the day sitting around and reviewing the situation from a tree or telephone pole, waiting for its prey to come by. It does not invest as much time soaring about on the active hunt as some of its close relatives do. Far from being a shy bird, it may well have profited from settlement of the eastern part of the continent; the change from forest to open fields for hunting and scattered woodlots for roosting and nesting seems to suit it perfectly.

The most noteworthy thing about all the buteos is their effortless, soaring flight. Like the vultures, they have broad, slotted wings that allow them to take the maximum advantage of updrafts. Thermal columns (streams of warm air rising from the ground) are especially useful to the soarers, who will swing round and round, climbing an invisible spiral staircase higher and higher, without ever a wingbeat. Other updrafts are the result of the topography of the country below. Cliffs and escarpments, and even large buildings, will cause prevailing winds to rush upward with enough force to support the circling birds. It is no accident that migrating birds of prey tend to be especially noticeable in places like Toronto's Scarborough Bluffs or Pennsylvania's Hawk Mountain.

When it is in flight, which is the time most of us see a hawk, this bird is clearly identifiable as a buteo by its soaring posture, long, broad wings, and wide tail. It is more slender than the related and commoner red-tailed hawk, and it shows a palish patch near the end of each wing. The broad-winged hawk is chunkier and smaller.

Pairs are said to remain together from year to year, often re-using the same nest each spring. They will give it a minimal clean-up and restoration, sometimes adding bits of new green foliage to the old sticks. Audubon said that his birds did not necessarily nest in exactly the same spot from year to year, but that they did return to the same copse or woodlot. The average number of eggs is three. Both sexes incubate, and care for the young birds. At this season the bird is exceptionally vocal. Its loud, piercing scream is readily imitated by blue jays.

There are five recognized races, or subspecies, of the red-shouldered hawk, of which the most attractive in my opinion is the pale, sandy-coloured bird of south Florida. In Canada, the red-shoulder is not widely dispersed; it is found only in southern Ontario and the south-western extremity of Quebec, and very occasionally in New Brunswick.

Length 21 inches. Wingspread 3¹/₂ feet.   Female, Hadlyme, Connecticut, January 7.

plate 12 — the sketch

BROAD-WINGED HAWK

Buteo platypterus

plate 12 BROAD-WINGED HAWK *Buteo platypterus*

Our smallest buteo is also undoubtedly the commonest, although its breeding distribution and habits are such that it may not be as frequently seen by most of us as some of its more familiar open-country relatives. This is a nesting bird of the dense woodlands; although it does occur in the west – east of the Rocky Mountains – its centre of abundance is the vast deciduous forest of the southern halves of Manitoba and Ontario, southern Quebec, and New Brunswick.

This is not a conspicuous bird at nesting time. It likes the leafy, covert surroundings of its woods; there is so much of that kind of country in eastern Canada that breeding pairs are hard to find. Broad-wings subsist during the summer on the mice, shrews, and other small mammals of the forest floor, and take good numbers of reptiles and amphibians, as well as insects. Its habitat being what it is, it follows that this is a somewhat more sprightly species than some of its close relatives, and no doubt it catches a number of small birds.

But if it is infrequently seen in spring and summer, in the autumn the broad-winged hawk is one of the most notable of Canadian birds. It appears in immense flocks during its southward migration. The only eastern buteo that leaves the country altogether in winter, its numbers begin to build up in early September for a flight which will take the birds to Central and South America. By the second to third week in September, the migration is in full stream. The hawks move out of the great eastern forests in a generally south-westerly direction until they reach the barrier of the eastern Great Lakes.

Buteos do not usually like to fly over extensive stretches of water; there are not enough consistent updrafts to accommodate their soaring flight. So, as they reach Lake Ontario, they turn west, following the lakeshore and the numerous bluffs, escarpments and other updraft-producing topographical features they need, towards the Niagara Peninsula. Very large flights are seen along the north shore of Lake Ontario from Cobourg westward. But it is when the masses of birds flow southwest along Lake Erie that the migration becomes truly spectacular. From Long Point westward, especially at a place called Hawk Cliff, near Port Stanley, Ontario, on a good day it is sometimes possible to see thousands upon thousands of broad-wings and substantial numbers of other species as well. On one fantastic day, seventy thousand birds were counted! The best dates, according to Earl Godfrey in *The Birds of Canada*, are from September 18 to 23. These are average dates, of course; because so much depends upon the weather, we can never be precisely sure when the flight will reach its peak.

In *Canadian Audubon* magazine, Olin Sewall Pettingill Jr. described the meteorological background. "In the fall, hawks tend to migrate south in greatest numbers on the second days after cold fronts when there are *steady* northwest to west winds and ample sunlight to produce thermals. . . To see hawks migrating in any appreciable numbers you must study weather maps and predictions so as to be present at places where the birds are known to pass when these wind and sunlight conditions prevail."

William W. H. Gunn, whose contribution to our knowledge of the influence of weather on bird migration has been the basis of much of the foregoing, is now plotting bird movements by means of radar (*see* ring-billed gull, *Plate 25*). The combination of a radarscope and a weather map is making fall hawk-watching much more predictable – and thus more people can enjoy it.

The broad-wing is identified by its small size (for a buteo), stocky build, and, in the adult, broad black-and-white bars on the tail. Young birds, which are sometimes numerous in the Florida Keys in winter, lack the distinctive tail pattern, but are pale under the wing, which has a dark border.

Length 15 inches. Wingspread 3 feet.   Male, Cedar Swamp, Coldstream, Ontario, April 29.

plate 13 — the sketch

MARSH HAWK

Circus cyaneus

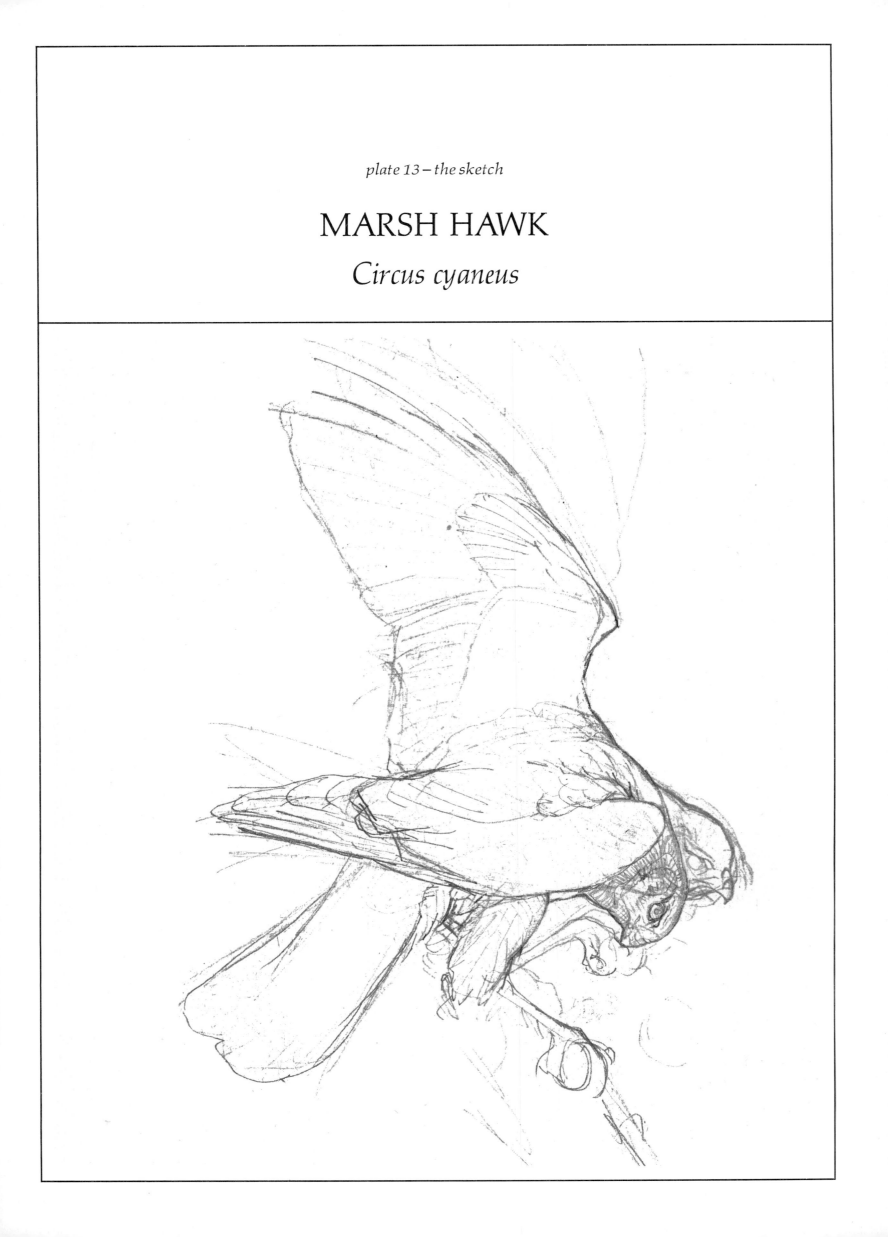

plate 13

MARSH HAWK *Circus cyaneus*

At a distance, the long-tailed marsh hawk looks superficially like a turkey vulture, with its long wings held in a typical V-shaped dihedral pattern, gently rocking back and forth, and doing a great deal of gliding. But there the resemblance ends; they are not related, even though some of their habits are similar. The best field mark for the marsh hawk is its shape, combined with a white rump patch.

In Britain, this fine bird of prey is known as the hen harrier. The harriers are a world-wide group of specialized hawks whose way of life is quite unlike those of their relatives. This is the only North American species. Harriers hunt by patiently quartering a marsh or grassy field at a very low elevation, watching for small mammals upon which they quickly pounce with long, slim legs. They catch snakes and amphibians too, and, occasionally, small ground birds such as rails, but marsh hawks aren't sufficiently swift or dexterous on the hunt to be significant bird-catchers. Sometimes they even run into trouble with mammals. Robert Trowern has told me of a marsh hawk which was repulsed and driven off by a large European hare in defence of her litter.

This hawk commonly eats carrion, a habit which has brought it a full measure of trouble. People are woefully prone to make instant judgements based on the slimmest circumstantial evidence. The harrier often eats game birds, for example, that may have died of wounds or of some other cause. The incautious (or prejudiced) observer rushes to the conclusion that these were the hawk's own victims, and promptly shoots it. A very great number of marsh hawks have been killed over the years by gunners under the mistaken impression that the birds compete with them for game. Except under the most unusual and rare circumstances, they do not. Another unfortunate result of scavenging can be the transference of pesticidal residues from the eaten to the eater. This is happening in our generation among peregrine falcons, bald eagles, and ospreys, all of which are seriously declining in numbers, as the result of ingesting toxic chemicals with their food. I believe that poisoning of its food resources is also affecting the marsh hawk.

Very few birds of prey habitually nest on the ground; the marsh hawk is an exception. The nest is well hidden. In the breeding season, the courting marsh hawks put on an extravagant aerial performance, described in *The Life of Birds* by Joel C. Welty. "(The male) plunges directly earthward from a great height, turning somersaults and uttering shrill cries during his descent. At other times, he impresses the female by performing an up and down roller-coaster flight, rising only a few metres above the ground and looping the loop and screeching on each downward plunge." The aerobatics of marsh hawks are not limited to courtship flights. In what might be termed "practice sessions," adult birds drop or pass prey items to the young in mid-air. For such a dogged hunter, the marsh hawk is a miraculous flier, when it cares to be.

This widespread species breeds from Alaska to the Maritimes, wherever there are suitable open marshes, prairies, and long-grass meadows. The male marsh hawk is blue-grey; the much larger female is brown, as are the young.

Length 20¹/₂ inches. Wingspread 3³/₄ feet.   Male, St. George, Utah, November 1.

plate 14 — the sketch

SPARROW HAWK

Falco sparverius

plate 14

SPARROW HAWK *Falco sparverius*

THIS species is another victim of the uniquely North American custom of calling all diurnal birds of prey "hawks." The sharp-shinned hawk (*plate 10*) is a true hawk; this bird is a falcon – our smallest. It is known as a falcon by its pointed wings, long tail, and strong, rapid wing-beats. At close range the falcons are also characterized by a singular tooth-and-notch arrangement in the bill.

Its colloquial name to the contrary, the sparrow hawk lives for the most part on large insects. Many people would like to see its name changed to "grasshopper falcon." An even preferable vernacular name might be "American kestrel," for clearly this bird is the opposite number of the very similar kestrels of the Old World. In addition to insects, its diet consists of the very smallest mammals, reptiles and amphibians, with some little birds thrown in. The size of the falcon (about that of a blue jay) limits its feathered prey to the small end of the scale.

This is easily our most common and best-known falcon. Unlike the others, which are essentially wilderness species, the little kestrel seems to have adapted itself admirably to man and human development. It has made itself completely at home around farms, villages and suburban residential areas, and even within cities. It seems that wherever there is a telephone pole or a television antenna from which the bird can survey its hunting grounds, it is perfectly content. Such look-out perches are very important. The bird will quietly and systematically survey its feeding territory, then launch itself swiftly into the air in pursuit of a delectable passing locust. At other times, especially over grassy areas, it will hover in mid-air as it checks the prey possibilities below.

Nesting is usually in holes in trees, sometimes in appropriate crevices in man-made structures. The birds will also come to artificial nesting boxes, but an old woodpecker digging is probably used most often. The average clutch of eggs is four. The young grow rapidly, and weigh as much as the adults in about three weeks. There is nothing like the high protein diet of a bird of prey to promote fast and healthy development in the early stages.

Since it is so common in so many parts of the country, it is not surprising that the sparrow hawk is often kept in captivity for purposes of falconry. Obviously, it is not capable of delivering anything significant in the way of game, but it can provide the beginner with a certain amount of interest and pleasure, and, presumably, experience. This may or may not be a positive thing. There is not much falconry practised in Canada, but in those places where there are nuclei of devotees they seem to attract a good deal of publicity, much of which is no doubt well deserved. But the publicity in turn attracts numbers of would-be new participants. The fear of many conservationists is that birds of prey falling into the hands of novices are not likely to survive the experience. Many young people attempt to emulate their heroes without going to them for proper guidance, and the danger is that a lot of people can go through a lot of captive birds in the course of a year. We have no birds of prey to spare.

The sparrow hawk breeds from coast to coast in southern Canada in summer, and is migratory. Some winter in the southernmost parts of the country, but much greater numbers spend the off-season in the south, most especially in Florida. In the Lake Okeechobee-Kissimmee Prairie country and in the Keys, Alexander Sprunt Jr. conducted random counts and "found them to occur at the rate of one a mile over a span of 13 miles." Over one 47-mile stretch of the upper Keys, my wife and I once counted 77 sparrow hawks: about one every three-quarters of a mile.

Length 10¹/₄ inches. Wingspread 2 feet.   Male, Islington, York Co., Ontario, January 26.

plate 15 — the sketch

RUFFED GROUSE

Bonasa umbellus

plate 15

RUFFED GROUSE *Bonasa umbellus*

THE ruffed grouse must be *the* game bird of broad-leafed and mixed forests in southern Canada, in terms of both numbers and popularity. A dashing, spirited, but wary fowl, it tests the skill and accuracy of gunner and photographer alike. Generally one's acquaintance with it is limited to a shattering split-second when the bird erupts like a land mine from the dead leaves of the forest floor, and immediately disappears with a loud whir of wing feathers. Then, absolute silence . . . and small likelihood of your seeing that bird again that day.

There are two distinct colour phases of the ruffed grouse, as there are in screech owls: a grey phase and a red phase. According to Earl Godfrey in *The Birds of Canada*, "the grey phase is commoner in interior western Canada, and both phases are more or less common in eastern Canada, but in extreme south-western British Columbia reddish-brown is predominant." The difference in colour is most obvious on the birds' tails.

Ruffed grouse prefer deciduous or mixed woodlands, although in summer they are more likely to be found in hardwoods, in winter, in conifers. There is little doubt that the bird is the beneficiary of clearing and fire, as is the white-tailed deer. Both prefer the new, lush, second-growth to a pure stand of mature forest. Since the grouse moves around very little in the course of a year, its home base must have enough variety in the way of vegetation to keep it going both winter and summer. Mixed forests are essential to its survival.

Despite its fame as a game bird, the ruffed grouse's greatest distinction is its unique spring mating performance. The birds are promiscuous, which means that individuals meet, mate, and go their separate ways. No pairs are formed. But it is the manner of the sexes' meeting which is so intriguing. The solitary male selects a prominent log or stump in the forest, where he takes an elevated position. He raises his wings and, slowly at first, then more and more rapidly, beats them against the air in a way that produces the effect of a muffled, swiftly accelerating drum-roll. The sound carries for a good distance through the forest, advertising the male's presence and preparedness. Receptive females within hearing range are attracted into his territory by the drumming, just as many female toads and frogs "home" on the singing of the males.

The female looks after the duties of nesting and incubation by herself, and usually builds at the foot of a stump or tree. But parental chores are not as onerous as they are in many families of birds; the precocial young are ready to forage for themselves within a day of hatching. The brood sticks together, however, for better protection against barred owls, foxes, and other potential enemies.

The grouse family is circumpolar in the northern hemisphere. Except for those that live in the most extreme climates, they are mostly sedentary, and do not migrate to any appreciable extent. For this reason they have had to develop adaptations to existence in cold weather. Ptarmigan, for example, have fully feathered feet and toes, which act as well-insulated snowshoes. A ruffed grouse's extremities are not feathered, but for the wintertime it grows thin, horny, pectinations along the sides of its toes. They do nothing for warmth, but they help in a locomotive sense as snowshoes. All species are densely feathered on the body, and all are extremely well camouflaged.

The ruffed grouse is found from the Yukon to Labrador and southward, in suitable habitat. It is subject to more or less regular cycles in abundance; populations will build to a peak over a period of years, drop off dramatically, and then slowly start building up again. The nature of this periodicity has yet to be completely understood.

Length 18 inches.   Male, Arden, Kennebec Tp., Frontenac Co., Ontario, November 20.
Female, De Grassi Pt., Simcoe Co., Ontario, May 24.

plate 16 – the sketch

BOBWHITE

Colinus virginianus

plate 16 BOBWHITE *Colinus virginianus*

No game bird can be better known or more popular in the eastern and southern U.S.A. than this little (7-ounce) quail. Not much in the pot, but apparently highly desirable in the field, it is one of the mainstays of the gunning industry in that part of the world. In Canada, however, it occurs naturally only in the south-westernmost part of Ontario, although (usually unsuccessful) attempts have been made to establish it in other parts of the country, such as southern British Columbia.

At one time the bobwhite was more widely distributed and more common in Ontario than it is now. As the forest lands were cleared, and wide brushy pastures and fallow fields took their place, the birds moved northward. The general planting of corn was a contributing factor. C. H. D. Clarke, of the Ontario Department of Lands and Forests, says that the bobwhite's range in our part of the world reached a maximum in the 1840s, but it is now limited to a handful of counties along the north shore of Lake Erie. The best place to see the birds in Canada today is between London, Ontario, and Lake St. Clair, where vast stretches of cornfields help them to maintain themselves during the difficult Canadian winter. Bobwhite are still reasonably dependable in that area.

No doubt the gradual shrinkage in the bobwhite's Canadian range following the initial invasion was the result of "clean farming." When farmland is meticulously manicured, there is no room for this quail. It must have sufficient brambly, rough, tangly places for cover and enough other ground vegetation to forage in. Clean farming also involves the removal of old or half-dead orchard trees and rotten fenceposts; this has contributed in great measure to the decline of other birds, such as the red-headed woodpecker and the eastern bluebird.

The bobwhite is easily identified by its diminutive size and its head pattern. In the adult male, the head markings are very conspicuous in black and white. Females and young birds are coloured in brown and buff. This is a gregarious animal which lives in groups or coveys, but there is a natural, self-imposed limit to the size of the flock. Coveys with a membership of up to about thirty are the maximum. Richard Pough says, "Each group makes its headquarters and roosts at night in good cover, ranging out to feed along brushy travel lanes for 300 to 400 yards and scattering in all directions when flushed. No covey allows others to trespass, nor does any covey accept additional members once the quota of 25 to 30 has been reached." There is only foraging space for so many birds in any one suitable area.

Bobwhite leave the coveys and form pairs for spring breeding. There is a very interesting pattern to their egg-laying. The female is said to lay her daily egg somewhat later each day, up to the point when it is occurring in the evening. Then, she will skip a day, and resume laying in the morning, until the clutch is complete. Both parents incubate the fifteen or so eggs for about three and a-half weeks. The young are precocial, able to move about and feed upon hatching. They are also born with the ability to voice the famous *bobwhite!* call of their species. This accomplishment is innate, not acquired, as experiments with young birds have demonstrated.

Length 10 inches.   Male, Ruscomb, Essex Co., Ontario, November 10.

plate 17 – the sketch

KING RAIL

Rallus elegans

plate 17 KING RAIL *Rallus elegans*

JOHN James Audubon discovered and named this fine big rail, which put him "one up" on his contemporary Alexander Wilson, who with other early naturalists of the time thought it to be the adult of the clapper rail, a related salt-marsh species. The king rail is a bird of the fresh-water marshland; to all intents and purposes the birds are opposite numbers in the two habitats.

The rails constitute a world-wide and cosmopolitan family; they are found on all continents (except Antarctica) and many oceanic islands. The expression "thin as a rail" no doubt came from the birds' remarkable ability to slink through narrow, seemingly impenetrable openings in their densely vegetated habitat. Our rails are all birds of marshlands, wet meadows, and such places. They are always secretive, sticking to the ground, rarely flying. That they are perfectly able to fly is obvious from their migratory travels, but fortunate is the observer who has ever actually seen any rail fly a significant distance. They swim efficiently, although this feat is rarely seen either.

The reluctance of these birds to reveal themselves was vividly illustrated in my first sight of a king rail in Toronto. The bird was on a little island in an artificial waterfowl pond in High Park, in the west end of the city. It was surlily skulking beneath a dense willow bush, the branches of which drooped well out over the water. At first, it was quite impossible to see, but then someone noticed its reflection in the still water, which was quite identifiable. We watched the bird at length, but only through its image. The steadfastly hiding rail hadn't though of *that!*

Difficult though it was to observe on that occasion, the king rail is not as a rule quite so retiring as many of its relatives. Given the right opportunity and a share of luck, you can sometimes see this species out in the open. But don't count on it. Its voice is always a good give-away: a sort of deep *bup-bup-bup*, with clicking variations on the basic theme. Like so many marsh birds, most rails are quite vocal.

The king rail is limited in distribution in Canada, and has occurred as a breeding bird only in a narrow belt along the north shores of Lakes Erie and Ontario from Lake St. Clair to Toronto. It is much more common in the eastern half of the United States, wintering in the south-east and along the shores of the Gulf of Mexico.

Length 17 inches.   Male, Louisiana, April 17.

plate 18 — the sketch

VIRGINIA RAIL

Rallus limicola

plate 18

VIRGINIA RAIL *Rallus limicola*

THIS bird looks to all intents and purposes like a miniature king rail, but it is much more common in Canada than its larger relative. In situations where size comparison is impossible, its grey cheeks readily identify the Virginia rail.

You will hear rails far more often than you will actually see one. The voice of this species sounds to me somewhat like that of a wood frog: a sort of metallic *ka-dick, ka-dick, or ka-duck, ka-duck*. Like all of its relatives, however, it has a wide repertoire, and many and irregular are the rail sounds you can hear in any large marsh after summer nightfall. On these occasions, it is accepted practice to lob small stones or sticks into the marsh. The rails, startled, will often respond with an identifiable cluck or other call, sending the birders home content. Lister Sinclair, with whom I have spent many such evenings, claims to be undisputed champion at scoring direct hits on the heads of rails in utter darkness. This must be what happens, he says, because he never hears anything further from them. Sinclair's most frequent victim is the elusive yellow rail.

Despite its name, the Virginia rail occurs all across southern Canada, except for mountainous and arid regions. Almost any sort of fresh-water marsh situation seems to suit it, including even brackish areas of light salinity. It winters from southern British Columbia through to the southern states and Central America. In view of its conspicuously weak and unimpressive flight on those rare occasions when it flushes, it is hard to comprehend how the bird could manage such long migratory journeys. Unquestionably it is a more efficient bird aloft than its summer behaviour would indicate.

The nest is built of woven marsh vegetation just a few inches above the water, and may contain eight or ten eggs. Downy young rails are black, which has sometimes led to erroneous reports of the black rail in Canada — a bird which, except on extraordinary occasions, does not occur in this country. Young Virginia rails are very active immediately after hatching, and can swim and dive, as well as run among the reeds. This is one of several species that occasionally, but not as a matter of practice, lay eggs in the nests of other birds.

Length 9¹/₂ inches.   Duncan, British Columbia, January 26.

plate 19 – the sketch

SORA

Porzana carolina

plate 19 ## SORA *Porzana carolina*

THE little sora's is the characteristic voice of marshes and other wetlands everywhere in Canada from the Mackenzie southward, except for western British Columbia and the northern part of Newfoundland. Its unmistakable descending whinny and querulous springtime whistle *ker-wee?* (Peterson) are among the first bird calls the beginner learns and retains with some confidence. This ubiquitous species is by far the most abundant of our rails. It is an adaptable bird, and seems to be able to find a living for itself in the most unpromising habitat circumstances. The merest little slough or tiny pond surrounded by green vegetation will attract and support a pair of soras. Large marshes are filled with them.

The sora's nest is constructed of grasses and leaves, cuplike, and fastened to the stems of taller marsh plants. Both sexes incubate the dozen or so eggs (a record of 18 exists) which are stacked in layers. The young are active swimmers at birth. One observer watched a young sora actually hatching: it rolled out of the egg, tumbled over the side of the nest, and swam away. At this stage, the young bird is a very peculiar sight. It is a roly-poly bunch of fuzzy black feathers accented by a brilliant patch of orange at the throat, and a yellow bill with a swollen red base.

During the spring and summer, soras live to a great extent on insects and other small marsh animals. In fall they turn vegetarian, and concentrate on the seeds of aquatic plants such as wild rice. On this high-calorie fare they fatten rapidly, building strength and stamina for their long trip southward, which may take them to the Gulf states and California, or to northern and central South America.

Our only other short-billed rail is the yellow rail, which is a bird of considerable mystery in Canada. It nests north to James Bay and the Mackenzie in shallow, short-grass marshes, and to the south has bred no more than thiry to forty miles north of Toronto, but its nest is rarely found. This bird, which is even smaller than a sora (7 inches), seems about as willing to flush as a mouse would be. The only sure way to see one is to catch it. It's best to try this at night. It has been accomplished (in my presence, exactly once) by getting a "fix" on a calling bird with two or more flashlights and then moving in on it. One night at the Holland Marsh, north of Toronto, my friend Jim Baillie caught one with a stab that would have done credit to a professional shortstop. I had heard them many times over the years, but that was only the second yellow rail I had ever seen. The yellow rail can be induced to reveal itself through its voice. You resort to the simple expedient of rapping two pebbles together in a special rhythm: *click-click; click-click-click.* As often as not, the bird will respond.

Soras require no such strategems. They are usually quite vocal, and if the observer waits long enough and patiently enough, they can be readily watched at twilight, whether morning or evening, as they carefully make their way around the edges of open water in search of their invertebrate food.

Length 8³/₄ inches.   Male, Toronto, Ontario, May 13.

plate 20 – the sketch

COMMON GALLINULE

Gallinula chloropus

plate 20   COMMON GALLINULE *Gallinula chloropus*

THE old name for this species was "Florida gallinule," which was inappropriate on at least two counts. First, the bird is cosmopolitan, and on this continent breeds northward into southern Ontario and extreme south-western Quebec. Second, *the* gallinule of Florida, which only rarely comes much farther north, is the purple gallinule, smaller and brilliantly coloured. Its range extends from the Gulf states to South America; occasional wanderers have turned up in Canada.

This is the Old World moorhen, one of the more widely distributed of birds, which occurs on all continents except Australia (where it is replaced by a relative) and, of course, Antarctica. Despite its somewhat chicken-like appearance and its occasionally ducklike behaviour, it is a member of the rail family that has taken more to the open water and, indeed, more to the drier land, than most of its marsh-dwelling relatives.

The common gallinule is identified by its dark body with white on the sides and under the tail, and by its red bill and frontal shield. Notice that its feet, like those of the rails, are not webbed or lobed. It swims perfectly well nonetheless, with a characteristic forward bob of the head at each stroke of the foot.

Few fresh-water marshes within its range are without the common gallinule, which seems to prefer areas that are broken with bits of open water. It will often make use of grassy or reedy ponds that are surprisingly small. The bird seems to be very good at looking after itself, and is not as fussy as some of its kin. It will make itself at home even within cities, if parks, golf courses, or other such areas provide even the least bit of appropriate habitat. In Europe I have noticed that this species is much more tame and fearless than it is in North America. Here, although it will live in close proximity with man, it is still shy. In Old World parks you will often see moorhens walking about on the grass like so many domestic pigeons.

Its long toes serve the gallinule well when it makes its way about a marsh. As it walks on the floating vegetation, from lily pad to lily pad, it reminds you of the more extreme jacanas of the tropics. When it is not picking its way along on foot, finding bits of vegetation and small animal life, the gallinule tips up like a dabbling duck, white bottom in the air.

The shallow nest is a flat affair made of marsh plants, sometimes partly floating, sometimes more firmly secured to the reeds and mud. Occasionally the bird has a delightful way of decorating its nest with bright objects such as pieces of flowers and bits of paper. During courtship, the male makes the best possible use of his limited adornments, displaying his brilliant red bill and flashing the snowy feathers beneath his tail. This species is known to go in for a form of symbolic nest-moulding during its courtship performance, in the course of which it may build a number of "dummy" nests. Some of these structures may be used as stand-by platforms at a later date, when the young hatch.

Ten or a dozen eggs are laid. The newly hatched chicks are covered with fluffy black down; they have red bills and a most peculiar, semi-naked, red "tonsure" on the top of the head. They swim immediately but are cared for by the hen for about a month, at which point she is preparing for her second brood of the year, and it is time for them to go their separate ways. By this time the young birds resemble the adults, but are duller and paler.

Gallinules are notoriously noisy birds. This is especially irritating in view of the fact that they are often so difficult to see. Many of their notes are quite chicken-like, and a large spring pond with every gallinule in full throat often sounds like a henyard. Other notes include a peculiar sort of "laughter," and sundry croaks and chuckles.

94   *Length 13¹/₂ inches. Wingspread 1³/₄ feet.   Male, S. Toronto, Ontario, July 6.*

plate 21 — the sketch

AMERICAN COOT

Fulica americana

plate 21

AMERICAN COOT *Fulica americana*

*A*LTHOUGH coots look superficially very like gallinules (or moorhens), notice especially the difference in their toes. A gallinule has long, slim toes like those of typical rails; a coot has extraordinary swollen lobes which remind you of the foot of the unrelated grebe. On the grebe, though the entire toe is lobed; with the coot, it is a *series* of independent lobes. The net effect is the same, however — better propulsion in the water. The white frontal shield is a good field mark; the gallinule's is red.

The coot is even more ducklike than the gallinule, when it is on the water. It swims and dives constantly; unlike most of the rail family it is very gregarious: it even consorts with flocking ducks to a great extent in the non-breeding season. In both structure and behaviour, it is the most aquatic of its family. Like a loon or a grebe, it has difficulty getting off the water in a hurry, and has to taxi long distances before it can become airborne. Often when you disturb a large flock of coots, they will scurry and splash their way across the water in a pseudo-take-off which never actually materializes; the birds just settle down again in another part of the lake or pond.

Coots are highly sociable at all seasons, but they are also notably aggressive and quarrelsome. Especially at breeding time, ponds and lakes are filled with the noise of their splashing, squawking, ill-tempered disputes. Here, the large sharplyclawed toes come into play as they lock in what William Whitehead so accurately described as "foot-to-foot combat." The sounds they make at these times are almost indescribable, but Richard Pough has summarized the descriptions as "croaks, toots, grunts, cackles, coughs, quacks, coos, whistles, squawks, chuckles, clucks, wails and froglike plunks and grating sounds." Which seems to pretty well cover it.

Safety in numbers seems to be the coot's policy in the winter, when very great flocks gather on lakes and other open water. At the approach of a potential enemy such as an eagle, hundreds of coots have been seen to jam together in a solid, compressed mass of slate-grey feathers, much in the way in which a large, loose flock of starlings will often "ball" at the sight of a hawk.

Coots are confirmed migrants, but do not as a rule travel in large flocks, as so many other birds do. H. Albert Hochbaum, of the Delta Waterfowl Research Station in Manitoba, says that coots travel singly, but that these individual birds make up large aggregations that apparently fly within hearing distance of each other. Sometimes they do it the hard way. In *The Migrations of Birds*, Jean Dorst reports upon a remarkable observation made by A. G. Prill, who "found American coots moving northward overland *(on foot!)* in the driest zones of an immense swampy area in Oregon during May, 1929. At least 8,000 birds marched past one spot in a morning, and Prill estimated that 10,000 or more crossed the area in four days." Other birds migrate on foot (the flightless Emperor penguin of the Antarctic has no choice in the matter); we are told that the wild turkey used to do so in the eastern part of this continent.

There are coots of one kind and another on six continents. Ours has a rather scattered breeding range in Canada, with its centre of abundance on the Prairies, but coots are found here and there in most southern parts of the country, from British Columbia to New Brunswick.

Length 15 inches. Wingspread 2¹/₄ feet.   Male, Toronto East, Ontario, May 20.

plate 22 — the sketch

KILLDEER

Charadrius vociferus

plate 22 KILLDEER *Charadrius vociferus*

THE most prevalent and familiar plover in Canada earned its vernacular name from one of its call-notes, and its specific name *vociferus* from the manner in which it delivers those calls. From British Columbia to the western Maritimes, all of southern Canada resounds to the shrill voice of the killdeer in spring and summer. Save possibly the robin, no native species is more conspicuous or more widely known.

There can be few if any indigenous birds (excepting, perhaps, the horned lark) that have been such obvious beneficiaries of the settlement of North America. Pastures, airports, cultivated fields, and flat waste areas of all kinds have provided optimum habitat for the adaptable killdeer, which must have increased substantially since Europeans arrived on this continent. It is unlike most shorebirds; it does not need water or watery places for nesting, and it can move to and make use of every scrape and scar the bulldozer and the earth-mover leave in their wake. Roadsides and railroad beds are used, and, occasionally, even parking lots.

The only thing a killdeer needs is a flat, open view. There is no nest as such; the merest hollow in the ground will do, with a few bits of grass for lining. The four eggs are buffy with dark markings. They are magnificently camouflaged and, in a sense, there is no real need for a nest; the colour of the eggs is their best concealment. It is interesting that if you do happen to spot them, and for any reason disarrange them in the nest, the adult killdeer will place them back in the right position again, with their narrow ends all pointing together. Presumably it is easier for her to cover them that way; they take up less room. Also, it is probable that there is less heat loss this way, or that it is greatly slowed down.

The adult killdeer itself is well camouflaged, despite the fact that it can be conspicuous when it chooses. If it remains perfectly still, the disruptive pattern of its markings (as opposed to the cryptic camouflage of the eggs) breaks up its outline, and the bird becomes just another scattering of small pebbles and their shadows. But when it is alarmed, all caution vanishes, and the excited bird uses voice and plumage, feathers and posture, in what appear to be frantic attempts to "distract" you from its nest.

The killdeer is world famous in this respect; it is the classic example cited in all reference to the distraction displays of birds. One must be careful, however, not to impute the wrong kind of motivation to the bird. It seems that this electrifying performance is the result of conflicting urges on the part of the killdeer: the urge to escape and the urge to protect its brood. The two tend to cancel each other out, with the result that the bird flutters about awkwardly and noisily, giving every appearance of being injured (the "broken-wing act"), and thus easily available prey. This act has the *effect* of distracting the attention of a predator from the nest or chicks to the adult bird — but it always stays well out of range. This mechanism, if we can call it that, certainly gets results, but we should not allow ourselves to think that the bird does it *consciously*.

Many birds do this type of displaying, most of them shorebirds, of which the avocet is possibly the most striking. But in my experience, the most unusual species to put on this act was a short-eared owl in the Galapagos Islands. With Roger Perry, I was photographing one of its young on the ground, when the adult owl launched a very elaborate "broken-wing" performance. When that failed to distract us from the young bird, the old owl sailed over and cracked me on the head. That worked.

The killdeer is an early arrival in spring, and late to leave in the fall. It is a hardy bird and a strong flier, and has turned up from time to time in Europe.

Length 10 inches. Wingspread 20 inches.   Female, Massett, Q.C.I., April 23

plate 23 — the sketch

AMERICAN WOODCOCK
Philohela minor

plate 23   AMERICAN WOODCOCK *Philohela minor*

You might say that the woodcock looks like a parody – or at least a grossly overdrawn and biased illustration – of adaptation and specialization to a narrow way of life. Certainly it has gone a long way for a sandpiper in committing itself to a limited field of activity: a life spent almost entirely on the ground in search of earthworms. But it must be said that no bird catches them more efficiently, and that where suitable habitat is available, the woodcock is a highly successful species.

This is not an obvious bird in the sense that a killdeer or a kingfisher is, and chances are that most people will never see one. But it is by no means rare, and if it is difficult to find at other times of the year, the sounds it emits in the springtime in its evening courtship display are easily identifiable. The woodcock inhabits alder swamps and other dense, moist thickets where the soil is soft and rich and the cover abundant. On the ground, its cryptic camouflage makes it almost impossible to see, but the ardour of springtime gives it away every time.

The male takes up station to sing in a small opening in an alder swale or other wet second growth. The sound he delivers falls somewhere between the nasal *beent!* of a common nighthawk and a human "raspberry" (the only man who can imitate it is Richard M. Saunders of the University of Toronto). After giving several of these notes, the bird takes to the air, circling a good distance upward, and then he slips, swoops and spirals downward, twittering gently as he descends. This elaborate and engaging performance continues all night long, if the moon is full, and only stops completely if the night is utterly dark. It serves to notify females, who are on adjacent territories of their own, that it

is time for mating. Firm pairs are not formed, and the birds may mate with various neighbours. Nesting and incubation are left to the females.

Structurally, the woodcock is perfectly designed for its specialty. If you are going to make a career of standing around with your bill deep in the ground, it pays to have a good range of eyesight. The bird's very large eyes are so placed in the skull that it has a greater range of binocular vision to the rear (where it needs it most) than it has to the front. The bill is long and slender, with a flexible tip; it can probe down to about three inches in soft soil in its never-ceasing pursuit of earthworms. A very short neck and diminutive legs have obvious value in keeping everything close to the ground.

Its diet of earthworms has alarmed many people who are interested in woodcocks. Earthworms and certain other invertebrates can store in their bodies substantial quantities of toxic pesticides, without being killed, A concentrated dose of the poison is then passed on to the bird that eats the worm. (The insidious chain from DDT to elm leaf to earthworm . to robin has been well documented.) It is feared that woodcock on their wintering grounds in the southern United States may in this way pick up more pesticidal residues than is good for them – as a species. The same may be true in the eastern part of their Canadian range, where so much aerial spraying for spruce budworm control has been carried out in the last decade. Studies of this question are in progress and, happily, research efforts are being intensified all the time.

The woodcock's range in Canada extends from south-eastern Manitoba across southern Ontario and extreme southern Quebec, through to the Maritimes and the lower tip of Newfoundland.

Length 11 inches. Wingspread 18 inches.   Male, Coboconk, Ontario, October 18.

plate 24 — the sketch

SPOTTED SANDPIPER

Actitis macularia

plate 24 SPOTTED SANDPIPER *Actitis macularia*

WHEREVER there is water in Canada, southward from the northern Yukon, Labrador and Newfoundland, you will find the spotted sandpiper – the most wide-ranging and commonest of its family. It seems that no pond, stream, lake, or river is without its complement of these beguiling little birds, whose thin whistles are heard from coastal tide pools to spruce-rimmed tarns of the far north. This is invariably the first sandpiper with which the new birdwatcher will become familiar, and it is one of the easiest to identify.

The conspicuous dark spots on breast and belly are seen only on adult birds in summer. Young, and winter adults, are clear white below. But the "spotty" is immediately recognizable in any plummage by its voice, its tilting, teetering behaviour on the ground, and its unusual flight. The voice is a thin, plaintively whistled *peep* or *pee-wee,* or a series of these. Whether standing or walking, the bird constantly tilts its rear end up and down in an amusing nervous action, the reason for which is not understood. This habit is so deeply ingrained in the species that young hatchlings begin to do it almost immediately. I have seen downy little chicks out of the egg only a matter of hours, tipping and bobbing every bit as much as the adults.

The flight is especially distinctive. When the bird is flushed (and you will often get very close to one before seeing it), it will give a few alarmed calls and then flutter away along the shore with bowed, stiffly vibrating wings held apparently below the horizontal; it soon comes to rest again and resumes its fidgety teetering. Although it seems a weak flier, it travels as far as central South America.

A number of observers have reported on the surprising underwater behaviour of this small sandpiper. Henry Marion Hall was one of these. In *A Gathering of Shorebirds* he says, "While fishing in the Housatonic River in Connecticut I once came upon a spotted sandpiper with a brood of chicks about one-third grown. I tried to catch one of the lively sprites but it dived from the margin of the stream and swam away underwater, using its small wings vigorously."

George M. Sutton wrote in *The Auk* of a similar experience with a grown bird. "When the bird first flushed, its wings were fully spread, and it was headed for the open water of the lake. Upon seeing me towering above it, however, it turned its course abruptly downward, and without the slightest hesitation flew straight into the water. With wings fully outspread and legs kicking, it made its way rather slowly along the sandy bottom, until it was about eight feet out, in water three feet deep. I pursued the bird, thinking at the time, strangely enough, that it was wounded. When I reached it, it tried to go farther but apparently could not. Bubbles of air came from its mouth, and air bubbles were plainly seen clinging to the plumage of its back. At the time it was captured its mouth, eyes and wings were all open, under water, and it remained at the bottom seemingly without difficulty. As it lay in my hands above water it seemed tired for a second or two, and then, without warning shook itself a little, leaped into the air, and with loud, clear whistles, circled off a few inches above the water to a distant point of land."

Spotted sandpipers rarely nest far from water. The nest is an informal matter – just a scrape or shallow depression in the ground, thinly lined with grass. It may be in the open, or under a stump or shrub. Four eggs are normally laid; they are buffish, with dark blotches and spots.

Length 7¹/₂ inches. Wingspread 13¹/₂ inches. *Female, Laird, Algoma Dist., Ontario, June 13.*

plate 25 — the sketch

RING-BILLED GULL
Larus delawarensis

plate 25

RING-BILLED GULL *Larus delawarensis*

In the first half of the 19th century, John James Audubon was under the impression that this was the commonest gull in North America. Although it may have been so at that time, this species is quite sensitive to disturbance, and many of the eastern colonies have been deserted in the intervening years. (But there are degrees of disturbance, and the birds' sensitivity could scarcely be blamed for the loss of a valued Montreal gull colony to the building of Expo 67.) However, nearly all the gulls seem to be prospering nowadays, for reasons not really understood, and despite its eviction from many favoured places in the east, the ring-bill has held its own, or even increased, elsewhere.

Gulls are very adaptable birds. Both this species and the California gull of the Prairies have learned to take advantage of agriculture. Great noisy flocks follow the farmers' ploughs and harrows, picking up insects and their larvae as they are exposed. And they are quick to take advantage of garbage dumps. This flexible opportunism of gulls so far as human activities are concerned has posed one of the great bird problems of our time – the increasing incidence of bird strikes on jet aircraft. A bird sucked into the intake of a jet engine can cause severe damage; birds fly at relatively low altitudes, and jet aircraft are especially vulnerable at takeoff and landing. Airports have attracted great numbers of gulls, right across the country, as airstrips are splendid places for sunning and loafing. Also, in the past, it has always seemed that the open spaces between runways and around airports were prime sites for the establishment of garbage dumps, or even for cultivation, both of which attract gulls by the thousands. The entire ecology of airports is now under study, so that the environment may be made less attractive to birds and thus somewhat safer for jets – and people.

The problem of birds at airports has led to other fascinating studies. William Gunn has been working intensively for several years on the detection of bird movements, including migration, by radar, so that when a major flight of birds is detected, aircraft traffic can be detoured appropriately. Not only air safety, but also ornithology is the beneficiary of such research programmes; radar and other technological devices are adding immeasurably to our knowledge of the ways of birds.

A strangely patchy breeding distribution in Canada is recorded for the ring-billed gull. It nests across much of the Prairies, in southern Ontario, the north shore of the Gulf of St. Lawrence, and in isolated spots in Labrador, Newfoundland, and elsewhere. We often are inclined to think of gulls as sea-birds, but they are coastal birds at best, never pelagic, and many of them, such as this species, breed in the middle of vast continents.

Although so many of our ring-bills live inland, good numbers are still coastal, and have a remarkable special adaptation for living in a salt water environment. Gulls and sea-birds have little or no access to fresh water in these places, so they are forced to drink sea water. But a bird's kidneys are even less efficient than those of a mammal in coping with salt water; a gull would have to excrete more than two litres of urine to deal with the salt in one litre of sea water, which would be a losing – and dehydrating – proposition. So, there has evolved an auxiliary system of salt disposal – a gland in the head which processes the bird's blood and gets rid of sodium chloride, which drips from the bill in highly concentrated solution. This gland exists in penguins, cormorants, gannets and others, as well as in gulls.

All gulls are consummate fliers; their motion in the air is graced with lightness, buoyancy, and manoeuvrability. They do a great deal of soaring and gliding, but such is their control that ring-billed gulls are expert flycatchers. Major insect hatches in farming country are frequently accompanied by wheeling, darting flocks of elegant ring-bills; it is one of the most attractive aerial performances of any of our birds.

Length 18¹/₂ inches. Wingspread 4 feet.   *Male, Little Lake, Barrie, Ontario, June 23.*

plate 26 – the sketch

COMMON TERN
Sterna hirundo

plate 26

COMMON TERN *Sterna hirundo*

THE grace and elegance of the common tern in flight are misleading; it appears a delicate, shimmering wisp of a bird, yet it sustains long-distance flights that demand unparalleled endurance – from central Canada as far as Mexico, the Falkland Islands, and the Straits of Magellan. In the Old World, it nests from Britain to Siberia and winters south to southern Africa, New Guinea, and the Solomons. One vagrant even made it to Fremantle, Western Australia, six months after having been banded as a chick in Sweden.

When we think about the amazing distances some of them travel, we might expect birds to get lost more often than they actually do. Much research has gone into the methods of orientation used by migrants, and common terns have frequently been subjects of experimentation. Jean Dorst tells of common terns released in Connecticut and Maine which "headed immediately south-east if the sun was visible, but not if it was hidden behind heavy clouds. This orientation can probably be attributed to the fact that terns on the east coast of the U.S.A. tend to fly south-east or east when they are lost or released over land. This may be an inherited tendency, for the birds are apparently aware that by flying in this direction they will eventually reach the coast. It is hard to account for all these facts on the basis of simple, visual landmarks. A real sense of orientation seems to exist, one linked with natural phenomena of which man remains unaware."

Migrating terns travel in large flocks, and it has been found that the inhabitants of a colony tend to stick together throughout the year. The young birds move south together in their first fall flight, and this association appears to continue through their lives. The same is true to a great extent of mated pairs, over three-quarters of which remained paired in the following season, in one breeding colony studied.

Tern colonies are notoriously frantic, helter-skelter, noisy places. The degree of nest-building seems to vary with the individual bird; some are attractive cups of dry grass, others are non-existent, with the two to four olive-brownish spotted eggs laid directly on bare rock. The eggs are so well camouflaged that they are surprisingly inconspicuous; the visitor must walk through a tern colony with great care. Adult birds will flutter and plunge about your head, dive-bombing angrily and making an ear-splitting racket. Although they threaten you fiercely, I have yet to be touched by a common tern, whereas the very closely related arctic tern has no qualms about striking your head sharply with its bill. It can be surprisingly painful.

Most colonies of common terns are situated on low, flat, rocky islands in both fresh water and salt. They will also use pebbly spits and other low-elevation places as long as they are sufficiently above high water and protected from mainland predators. The birds have lost so many nesting sites in our time that when they occupy a new one it is noteworthy. That this happens at least occasionally, even with today's general scarification of the landscape, was illustrated recently. Dredging and filling associated with the "development" of Toronto Island resulted in the creation of a long, low bed of sand and gravel fill. Almost as soon as this new, artificial habitat appeared, the terns moved in – the first nesting of this species ever recorded in the Toronto area. Such is the readiness of wild birds to take advantage of whatever crumbs we see fit (even inadvertently) to throw them.

Length 15 inches. Wingspread 2¹/₂ feet. Male, Favourable Lake Mine, Ontario, July 21.

plate 27 — the sketch

MOURNING DOVE

Zenaidura macroura

plate 27 MOURNING DOVE *Zenaidura macroura*

With the exception of the introduced Old World rock dove (domestic pigeon), the mourning dove is the most numerous and widely ranging of its family in North America. It nests from coast to coast in Canada, but only in a rather slim belt in the southernmost part of the country. That this coincides nicely with the bulk of human settlement may be more than sheer accident. The mourning dove is one of the comparatively few forms of native wildlife to which human occupation of the continent could well have been a positive advantage.

Ideal mourning dove habitat is open, sparse meadows and pastures for feeding, with woodlots and hedges for cover and nesting. Agricultural development has created an abundance of such country. Ironically, some soil-mining on our part does not bother the bird; it rather likes its grassland to have lots of bare spots. Weed seeds are staples, and we have managed to produce plenty of *them*. Also, mile after mile of wide cornfields have added to the availability of winter food and cover, and in southernmost Ontario good numbers of the birds manage to over-winter. They are not reluctant to live in city parks; their fearlessness and willingness to take up permanent residence at such close quarters with man has undoubtedly built up their numbers in the last few human generations.

A dove's nest is a somewhat unattractive and insubstantial construction of small twigs, nearly always on a horizontal branch well above our eye level. It is built solely by the female, with materials provided by the male. Two pure white eggs are incubated by both parents for about two weeks. The new hatchlings, like those of all pigeons and doves, are fed for the first little while on "milk." This highly nutritious substance, which is provided by both parents, is strikingly similar to the milk of mammals, protein-rich and high in fats. It is produced by an upsurge in the production of cells in the lining of the crop, which are then shed in great quantities and fed to the young in a form that resembles curds. For the first few days this is the only food the nestlings take; then they graduate to regurgitated masses of small weed seeds and the more familiar pigeon mast. The young are brooded almost continuously until they are surprisingly large.

In a quantitative sense the mourning dove is an extremely important game bird in the southern United States; the annual kill runs into millions. The bird is a swift, whistling flier, and no doubt tests a gunner's speed and control, but I have often wondered at the rewards involved in shooting a four ounce bird. After cleaning, it would hardly seem worth the effort; I suspect that substantially fewer may reach the table than are annually shot down. An open season on mourning doves was declared one year in Ontario, but such was the public outcry that it was not continued. In the northern parts of their range, mourning dove populations have a difficult enough time getting through the winter without having to endure a prior decimation in an autumn shooting season.

The bird's name derives from its voice: a mournful, repetitious cooing that has a strange ventriloquistic quality. In appearance it is superficially like (though much smaller and duller) the extinct passenger pigeon, which paid with its existence for the greed and ignorance of the second half of the 19th century. Paradoxically, settlement destroyed the one species and helped the other.

Length 12 inches.   Male, Christchurch Parish, South Carolina, May 11.

plate 28 — the sketch

YELLOW-BILLED CUCKOO

Coccyzus americanus

plate 28 YELLOW-BILLED CUCKOO *Coccyzus americanus*

THAT such a strikingly handsome bird as this should be so infuriatingly secretive and shy is one of the crosses the birdwatcher must learn to bear. Occasionally you will glimpse one in flight, in which case the large white tips on the tail feathers combined with a reddish flash on the wings will identify it. But make sure you recognize it quickly; it will immediately dart into the most impenetrable thicket, where it will skulk immobile for an eternity, crouching round-shouldered in the deepest shadow. A rare glimpse at close quarters will reveal the yellow lower mandible, though viewing at that range is difficult with cuckoos.

The world-wide family of cuckoos is a very large one, comprising some 130 species, and including such North American birds as roadrunners and anis. The best-known member of the family seems to be the European cuckoo, whose voice is one of the few bird songs that nearly everybody recognizes. This and certain other Old World cuckoos are parasitic: they lay their eggs in the nests of other birds, banking on the maternal instincts of the foster-mother to see the young cuckoo on the wing. This practice has become so specialized that in some areas the eggs of the cuckoos have come to resemble those of their favourite victims. Even more remarkable is the fact that more than one "clan" of cuckoos can co-exist in the same locality, each "clan" producing eggs resembling those of its usual host. New World cuckoos are not parasitic as a rule, although there are occasional instances of it in this species. It has even been known to lay in the nest of its cousin, the black-billed cuckoo, which is also known to have returned the compliment.

This is a more southern bird than the black-billed, and its range in Canada is correspondingly restricted: the extreme southern portion of British Columbia, southern Ontario, and the bottom tip of New Brunswick. Cuckoos appear to vary a great deal in numbers from year to year and, in spring migration in the east, one year one species will predominate, the next year, the other. But that is a local condition; the black-billed cuckoo ranges much more widely in Canada as a breeding bird.

Cuckoos are known wanderers, and often seem to be caught up in autumn storms. They are not the strongest fliers in the world, preferring to feed in dense shrubbery near the ground, and rarely moving any distance; perhaps their chances of being carried by weather systems are greater than those of the more aerial birds. This species has been recorded in the Maritimes and Newfoundland, and has even turned up in Europe.

Young cuckoos are fantastic creatures; like newly hatched pelicans and cormorants, they seem to advertise their reptilian ancestry more blatantly than most birds. Lester Snyder and Shelley Logier found a yellow-billed cuckoo's nest at Long Point, Ontario. "The young were quite active when disturbed. They scrambled about the bush, using the wings and bill for climbing. One young which was brought to our camp demonstrated a remarkable reptile-like behaviour. When it was placed on the table and one reached to pick it up, it erected its somewhat horny plumage and emitted a buzzing hiss like the sound of bees escaping from a tunnel in dry grass. This performance was certainly unbirdlike in all respects." C. E. Bendire described the newly hatched young as "repulsive, black, and greasy-looking creatures, nearly naked, and the sprouting quills only add to their general ugliness." From such modest beginnings comes one of our most elegant birds.

Length 12¹/₄ inches. Male, Southport, North Carolina, May 11.

plate 29 – the sketch

BLACK-BILLED CUCKOO
Coccyzus erythropthalmus

plate 29 BLACK-BILLED CUCKOO *Coccyzus erythropthalmus*

ACROSS forested southern Canada east of the Rocky Mountains to the Maritimes, the black-billed cuckoo is the most familiar representative of its family. It is especially noticeable in years of forest tent caterpillar infestation; this and the yellow-billed are among the very few birds that will eat these seemingly unpalatable creatures. They also devour other kinds of hairy caterpillars with evident relish, including the colonial web net builders of wild cherry trees. The stiff spines of their victims do not seem to bother the birds, even though their stomachs are frequently lined with "fur" as the result.

In its furtive, stealthy behaviour this species is essentially like the yellow-bill. The only person I know who can consistently spot a hiding cuckoo is my wife Peggy, who has never satisfactorily explained her technique. The bird sits tight in a dense bush, where its browns and olives blend astonishingly with the shrubbery around it. Sometimes, if it is convinced that you cannot see it, it will allow an unexpectedly close approach. But, once you pass the invisible tolerance line, it will slip sinuously away to another hiding place. The best evidence of its presence, as with the other species, is its voice. In this bird, it consists of a very long string of low notes on the same pitch, delivered in groups in rhythmic sequence. The call of the yellow-bill is more hollow and woody, beginning with a series of clucks that gradually become more drawn-out and slower, dropping off at the end. It sometimes sounds for all the world like a pied-billed grebe.

In *The Birds of Minnesota*, Thomas S. Roberts reported on the peculiar nest-feeding behaviour of this species. "When the old bird returns, the food, which is very likely to be *live* caterpillars, is concealed in the throat. As a nestling raises its head with open mouth and rapidly vibrating wings, the parent thrusts its bill deeply into the open maw and the young bird grasps securely the smooth bill of the old bird, in which action it is greatly aided by several soft papillae or disks in the roof of the mouth. Then, with a slow, pumping motion, the squirming caterpillars are transferred with some difficulty from one mouth to another. The process is a slow one, the birds being attached a minute or more and the transfer aided, apparently, by a sucking effort on the part of the nestling." No doubt the spots in the mouth of the young bird also act as targets or "releasers" for feeding activity by the parent.

Nestling cuckoos look amazingly like prickly little lizards. They are covered with stiff spines, which are the sheaths of feathers forming inside. These sheaths break open almost simultaneously in just a matter of hours, and the bird removes them with its bill. In half a day the bird is transformed from a kind of reptilian urchin into a proper young cuckoo (minus the long tail, which takes a little while longer).

Migrating black-billed cuckoos fly as far south as Colombia, Ecuador, and northern Peru. Sometimes they are recorded in Europe.

Length 11³/₄ inches.   Male, Southport, North Carolina, May 16.

plate 30 – the sketch

BARN OWL

Tyto alba

plate 30

BARN OWL *Tyto alba*

THE "monkey-faced owl" has been the very model for spine-tingling folklore over many centuries. In its appearance, voice, nocturnal habits and most especially its choice of nesting sites (abandoned buildings, belfreys, lofts, ruins, etc.) it does all the things that you *expect* an owl to do. And it does them all surpassingly well. In Canada, it is restricted as a breeding bird to the extreme south-western corner of British Columbia and southern Ontario from Niagara Falls westward. Barn owls of several sorts are found all over the world, but this is the only representative of its family in North America.

Barn owls are quite different from other owls in anatomy and general appearance. The long legs and skinny toes (they look that way because they are more lightly feathered than those of other owls), the small eyes and peculiar shape of the face are all good field marks for this species. Seen in flight from below, the bird appears to be pure white, and even for an owl, the head looks extraordinarily large.

Owls have remarkable eyesight, but they also have incredibly acute hearing. Experiments with this species have shown that the bird's directional hearing enables it to find a prey target accurately by ear alone, in total darkness. It is said to hear most efficiently at frequencies above 9,000 cycles per second. The squeak of a mouse elicits an immediate reaction, as I have found by imitating the sound at night and drawing a barn owl to within a foot or two of my car window.

This bird is very traditional in its nesting sites, using the same place year after year. It does not build a conventional nest, but the debris of many seasons gradually accumulates, producing a kind of soft covering for the floor of a disused attic, church tower, or other suitable location. For many years barn owls nested (hopefully, they do yet) in a silo near Queenston, Ontario. A long ladder allowed access to the nest; the floor surrounding it was littered to a depth of several inches with felt-like pellets of regurgitated indigestible material, and the bones and feathers of small prey species.

The eggs are pure white, and there may be between five and ten or more. Unlike birds such as ducks, which do not begin incubation until the entire clutch of eggs is laid, owls start to incubate with the first. The result is that the young birds vary dramatically in age and size. In years when food supply is ample, all or most of them survive. When the squeeze is on in terms of food, frequently the younger, smaller birds die of starvation or are actually eaten by older and stronger siblings. Barn owls dispose of a great many mice; half-grown young have been observed being fed as many as ten prey items per night. The old birds are kept busy while the young are growing, which can be at almost any time of the year. Barn owls have no defined nesting season.

Since this owl is so adaptable and flexible in the sites it will use for nesting, it is perhaps surprising that it has not dispersed more generally in Canada. An interesting speculation has been made that its spread through New York State in the past few decades was due at least in part to the arrival of electricity, and most especially, of electric refrigeration. As all the old ice-houses fell into disuse, the barn owls moved in!

The most remarkable concentration of barn owls in my experience (even including the numbers in the Florida Keys in winter) is in Guayaquil, port city of Ecuador. Here, the banks of the Guayas River seethe with rats; statuary and other projections on downtown buildings are homes for barn owls, which make a prosperous living from the squalid conditions below.

Length 18 inches.   Male, Corpus Christi, Texas, February 2.

plate 31 – the sketch

SCREECH OWL

Otus asio

plate 31

SCREECH OWL *Otus asio*

SEVERAL species of owls have "horns," or tufts of feathers, on their heads, but the others are much larger than the little screech owl. It can only be confused with the rare flammulated owl of southern British Columbia, but that bird has dark, not yellow, eyes. The name of the bird is quite absurd; there *are* owls that screech, scream, and shriek, but not this one. Its voice is a low, quavering whistle with a strange tremulous quality; oddly enough, it is easily imitated.

The most singular thing about this small, attractive owl is that it comes in two colour phases. Adult birds may be either grey or reddish: this coloration is permanent, yet it has nothing whatever to do with age, sex, or any other consideration. Both colours may occur in one brood, and mated pairs may be the same or different colours. In my experience the red phase seems to be more common to the south, where the two colours are found about equally. In Canada, the grey phase predominates. The red bird does not occur at all in British Columbia, but there is a darker, brownish subspecies there.

No other Canadian owl habitually and commonly takes up residence in cities. The screech owl must have trees for nesting, usually large ones with natural cavities or old woodpecker holes, and a little bit of open ground to hunt in, but otherwise its requirements are few. I well remember a pair of nesting screech owls in an old oak tree on the University of Toronto campus. One of the birds was so aggressive to passers-by that Professor Richard Saunders, who had to pass that tree on the way to his lectures took to carrying an umbrella with which to protect himself.

The food habits of screech owls, like those of all birds of prey, vary with the seasonal abundance of their victims. This is a small bird that takes proportionately small prey. It is always on the lookout for frogs and mice, of course, but in season it will catch great numbers of moths, June bugs, grasshoppers, crickets, and such small fry. In winter, when times are somewhat harder, the sedentary owls must work a little more strenuously, and they often turn to bird-eating. But there are lots of house sparrows to keep them going in the cities, and the owls' effect on the native bird population must be minimal.

Generally the only glimpse you get of a screech owl at home is of its little face and "ears" framed in the opening of its nesting hole in a tree. Even when you cannot see the bird, if you know the hole is inhabited, sometimes a few sharp raps on the bark will prompt it to peer out at you. If the bird is caught away from home, it will sit motionless as close to the trunk as possible, relying on its excellent camouflage. If it thinks it is being observed, it will perceptibly shrink in girth and stretch in height, stiffly erecting its head tufts in an apparent attempt to become a part of the tree itself.

In North America, screech owls range from Alaska to Mexico; in Canada, they nest regularly only in south-western British Columbia, the south-eastern Prairies, and southern Ontario.

*Length 10 inches.   Male, Ellendale, Delaware, March 24.
Male, Dagsboro, Delaware, January 18.*

plate 32 — the sketch

BARRED OWL

Strix varia

plate 32

BARRED OWL *Strix varia*

Its round, tuftless head and dark eyes distinguish this large fluffy owl from all others except the scarce spotted owl of south-western British Columbia, a much darker bird with no stripes on the lower part of its body. The barred is a fairly common owl, as owls go, throughout the forested parts of southern Canada, from central British Columbia to the Maritimes. This is the northern limit of its range, which extends through the United States to Central America.

This is a woodland species that only occasionally ventures into the cities. It prefers dense stands of deciduous forest and, for such a large bird, makes its way among the trees with remarkable finesse. It has a mild and gentle disposition for a big owl, and rarely tackles such formidable prey as does the great horned owl. It limits itself to things the size of frogs or lizards, with mice the major part of its diet, but it is sprightly enough to pick up grouse chicks occasionally. At night I have seen one hawking in mid-air at moths attracted to a floodlight. Sometimes it catches and eats lesser owls.

The usual voice of the barred owl is distinctive, and easy to imitate. It consists of a series of hollow hoots in a certain rhythm: *Who cooks for you? Who cooks for you-all?* The bird will often call in the daytime (at a distance it sounds like a dog barking), and if you respond, sometimes it will come up to you. Around the nest, the birds give a variety of other deep-throated notes.

Nesting is usually in a hollow tree, but the bird has also been known to use the abandoned nests of hawks or crows, as a great horned owl does. Once Fred K. Truslow, the distinguished bird photographer, showed me a barred owl's nest on the ground in Florida's Everglades National Park, but that is exceptional. Birds have been known to return to the same nest, or to the immediate vicinity, for as long as twenty to twenty-five years, according to Alexander Sprunt, Jr.

Since barred owls can often be approached quite closely, they are frequent victims of the traditional prejudice which for so long has surrounded all birds of prey. A boy with a .22 rifle finds a big owl a fetching target, and not enough parents yet recognize the positive, beneficial influence of predatory animals in the wildlife community. The barred owl is an especially inoffensive animal, weakly equipped for killing, which does no harm whatever and a great deal of good. It is legally protected now in most parts of the continent, which it richly deserves, but many still fall before the weapons of the uninformed and the indifferent. We remain a frontier people in many ways.

Length 20 inches.   Male, West Point, New York, January 28.

plate 33 — the sketch

SAW-WHET OWL

Aegolius acadicus

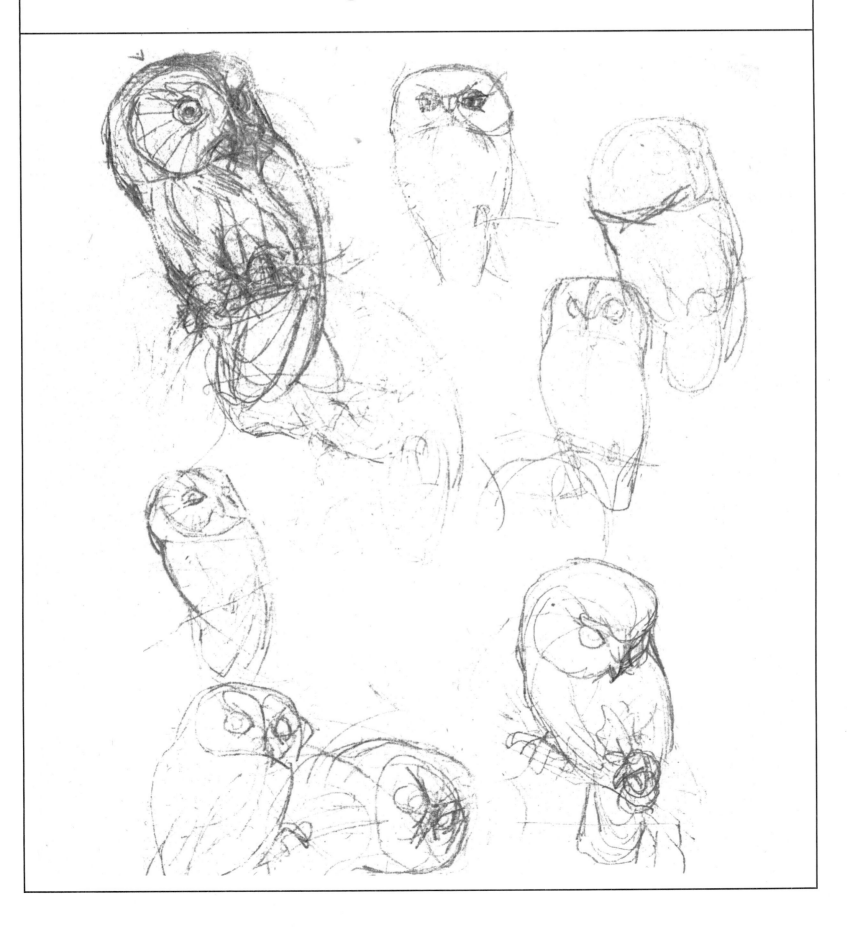

plate 33 SAW-WHET OWL *Aegolius acadicus*

THE exceptional tameness of this little owl is well known. It can readily be approached, touched, and even caught in the hand. I have done so on many occasions. Before a general "clean-up" of Toronto's lakeshore took place several years ago, numbers of saw-whets used to rest in dense willow jungles during their fall migration. Many were banded, but many more were killed or injured by unthinking children. Some of these disabled birds were caught and cared for by local birdwatchers.

One such bird in particular which I took home with me shed some interesting light on owls in general. This one had suffered a broken leg and a damaged wing, both of which healed in due course, and eventually the bird was as good as new. I lived at that time in an unusually dark and almost windowless apartment; the owl had the free run of it. As night came on, it would perch on a select lampshade in the hall. Then, as everyone went to bed and began turning out lights, it would follow from room to room until the last bulb was extinguished. At this point, the trouble would start. In complete darkness, with no light source at all, the bird would panic, fluttering about in the hall until someone would get up and turn on its lamp. There it would perch contentedly all night long. Of course owls can see no better in complete darkness than we can; their famed eyesight is a matter of being able to make do with the absolute minimum of illumination.

My bird did very well on a diet of liver and chicken heads; after a day or so of forced feeding it ate readily. It did so well, in fact, that when the time came for its release it was quite unwilling to leave. I repeatedly turned it loose from the back porch, but each time it would slip back through the kitchen door before it shut. Only after I threatened it with a broom did it finally take its leave. The children of the house missed it, and would mournfully gaze at its favourite perch, an empty quart soda bottle on top of the refrigerator, which remained for some time as a souvenir. (The bird's lampshade had long since been dealt with.)

The name of this bird derives from one of the noises it is reported to make, which has been likened to the sound of a saw being filed. My own experience with its voice is limited to one occasion. Fenwick Lansdowne and I once heard a saw-whet in Ontario's Muskoka country, which gave an interminable series of soft metallic *pings* somewhat like the sound of water dripping.

The saw-whet owl is found in deep woodlands from coast to coast in southern Canada. Its range somewhat overlaps that of the more northern and quite similar boreal owl. The latter bird is larger (about 10 inches), with a yellow bill and a dark border around its facial discs. Both nest in holes in trees, the saw-whet usually in the abandoned diggings of flickers and other woodpeckers. Like those of other owls, the five or six eggs of the saw-whet are white.

When they are not nesting, these attractive little birds like to roost in dense shrubby tangles, or in evergreens. Usually they move as close to the centre as possible, often surprisingly near the ground. They are easy to miss; I can remember passing and repassing some small conifer a number of times in the course of a day, only to eventually spot the bird, which had undoubtedly been there all the time.

Small owls are frequently preyed upon by larger owls, and this must be the fate of a good many saw-whets (and may account for their willingness to take their chances close to the ground). Bird banders in Toronto who had ringed several of these birds in migration once found one of their saw-whet bands only a day or two later in the regurgitated pellet of a long-eared owl.

Length 8 inches.   Male, Princess Anne, Maryland, December 17.

plate 34 — the sketch

WHIP-POOR-WILL
Caprimulgus vociferus

plate 34 WHIP-POOR-WILL *Caprimulgus vociferus*

IN south-eastern woodlands, few summer sounds are more commonplace than the voice of this species, and yet there are not many familiar birds that are less frequently seen. Commencing at twilight, and continuing late into the night, the male whip-poor-will endlessly repeats the monotonous and far-carrying song from which it gets its name. The bird may call scores or even hundreds of times without stopping. E. H. Forbush has reported upon the rare patience of John Burroughs, who "made a count which so far as I know exceeds all others. He records that he heard a bird 'lay upon the back of poor Will' 1,088 blows with only a barely perceptible pause here and there, as if to take breath."

Caprimulgus means "goatsucker." A fantastic folk-tale persisted for many generations to the effect that birds of this family descended upon flocks of goats at nightfall to drink their milk. It is not difficult to deduce how the legend was born: the crepuscular and nocturnal habits of this strange, swift, silent-flying bird were peculiar enough, and its enormous mouth seemed made to order for sucking milk. But, in fact, the birds live entirely on invertebrates.

The whip-poor-will is superlatively adapted to its way of life. The bill is quite small, but the open mouth is immense; like a kind of flying funnel, it takes in hapless low-flying moths. Bristles about its gape presumably widen the scope of the trap. On the wing, the bird is surprisingly deft and manoeuvrable, thanks to its long wings and tail. Its dense, soft feathers are very like those of an owl; the result is soundlessness aloft and superb camouflage when the bird is at rest. The legs and feet are small, short, and quite weak, to the point that goatsuckers cannot perch across a twig as other birds do. They must rest horizontally along a branch large enough to accommodate the entire body. Very often they rest directly on the ground.

No nest is built. The two eggs, which may be white, or spotted and blotched, are laid on the ground in the dry leaf litter of the forest floor. Winsor Marrett Tyler, in A. C. Bent's *Life Histories,* gives an appealing description of the downy nestlings. "The little whip-poor-will chick, hatching out from an invisible egg, finds itself lying on the ground, with dead leaves all about. The dead leaves look like the chick, and the chick looks like the dead leaves; no one can tell them apart; practically the chick *is* a dead leaf, and, although hatched, it is still invisible, just as it was when hidden in the egg."

The food of the whip-poor-will consists mostly of those flying insects that are abroad at night – moths, mosquitoes, and others, also crickets and grasshoppers. The bird has been seen to forage awkwardly on the ground, but this behaviour must be exceptional, in view of its anatomical limitations.

Although it is anything but rare, the whip-poor-will is not as abundant as it once was in the region. Its need for dry, well-drained hardwood forests has resulted in its gradual decline, concurrent with that of its essential habitat. C. H. D. Clarke has pointed out that the bird cannot tolerate the presence of large grazing animals in its woods, and as cattle have been turned into so many of our farm woodlots, a very great deal of otherwise perfectly suitable whip-poor-will environment has been at least temporarily destroyed.

Length 9³/₄ inches.   Highland Falls, New York, May 31.

plate 35 — the sketch

COMMON NIGHTHAWK

Chordeiles minor

plate 35   # COMMON NIGHTHAWK *Chordeiles minor*

Far from being a hawk, this bird is a goatsucker or nightjar, a relative of the whip-poor-will. But, unlike most other members of its family, is just as likely to be seen in the daytime as at night. The nighthawk is another of the small band of birds that seem to have been helped by human settlement of this continent. Unlike the whip-poor-will, which needs for its nesting woodlands with a carpet of dry leaves, this species likes flat, open, rocky or gravelly places. The pebbled roofs of modern buildings have created a wealth of nighthawk habitat – probably much more than was available to them before our time. As the result, every city and town in Canada from coast to coast (except for Newfoundland) has its full complement of noisy, conspicuous nighthawks.

The birds are especially evident during migration, when large loose flocks move during the daytime and early evening. One of the greatest congregations I have ever seen was on a late-August day in Regina, Saskatchewan, when a vast number of birds flowed like a flat plume of smoke across the prairie sky. (As I write this, in Toronto on Labour Day weekend, my son Peter has just come in to report a flock of at least 100 nighthawks circling overhead just before dusk, right on schedule.)

Nighthawks customarily fly and feed at much greater altitudes than whip-poor-wills, which do their hunting close to the ground. They live entirely on flying insects, which they pursue with darting, erratic, but highly controlled aerobatics. Examination of nighthawk stomachs has been revealing: some contained as many as fifty different species of insects. One bird has eaten 2,175 flying ants. Another contained 34 May beetles (June bugs), a substantial load for a bird of its size.

In season, the nighthawk is a notably vociferous creature. Its call, a loud, somewhat grating and nasal *beent!* is one of the most familiar sounds of summer evenings in the city (yet surprisingly few people seem to be aware of its source). Another sound, this one mechanical rather than vocal, is produced by the male bird in the course of his courtship performance. He plummets swiftly earthward, then swings aloft again very abruptly; the air rushing against his feathers produces the avian version of a sonic boom. In the early 19th century, Alexander Wilson, pioneer American bird student, guessed that the sound was made "by the sudden expansion of his capacious mouth." After more careful observation, his contemporary and sometime competitor, John James Audubon, came to the right conclusion, calling the sound a "concussion."

The nighthawk is readily identified in flight by the striking white patches on its long, pointed wings. At rest, the wingtips are longer than the tail (the whip-poor-will's are shorter). Should there still be any doubt, choice of habitat is nearly always diagnostic.

In the American Southwest there is another species of nighthawk which is somewhat smaller and flies very close to the ground. Since all these birds are completely dependent on flying insects, in our latitudes they must migrate. The nighthawk winters throughout most of South America.

But not all goatsuckers migrate. The related poor-will of the far west has been discovered to answer the winter food problem as some mammals do – by hibernating. Thus far, it is the only bird in the world known to have undertaken such an unbirdlike inactivity. It seems that cool weather, as it cuts down on the insect supply, reduces the bird to a kind of torpidity which is the accepted rule among reptiles and amphibians. From medium to deep torpor one might suppose that it is a relatively short step to hibernation, but it is a giant leap for a bird. All the goatsuckers are extremely well feathered and insulated, however, as was demonstrated by a female nighthawk that was able to hold the temperature of her eggs to a constant 46°C even though the gravel roof around her soared to a blistering 61°C (142°F).

Length 10 inches.   Male, 85 mile, Cariboo, British Columbia, July 4.

plate 36 — the sketch

CHIMNEY SWIFT

Chaetura pelagica

plate 36 ## CHIMNEY SWIFT *Chaetura pelagica*

*A*LTHOUGH an overwhelming majority of birds can fly to at least some extent, and most of them well, few can match the almost total commitment of the swifts to the air. Except for the need to deposit their eggs on something of substance, they are wholly emancipated from the terrestrial world. Feeding, drinking, even mating, are accomplished on the wing. Swifts are characterized by their tiny bills and feet, enormous mouths, cigar-shaped and apparently tailless bodies, and their stiffly tapered, often bowed wings. But they are especially and immediately recognizable by their flight, the fastest in the bird world – erratic, volatile, darting. The wings often give the appearance (but only the appearance) of beating alternately. This jagged pattern of flight, with wings set stiffly and much planing between series of beats, is diagnostic of the swifts.

Before pioneer days in North America, chimney swifts nested in hollow trees, and no doubt many still do, although I have never seen a nest of this species in anything but a man-made structure. Just as flat roofs have been so beneficial to the nighthawk, and farming to the killdeer and mourning dove, so the advent of chimneys opened up new and ideal possibilities for the swifts. But in addition to the millions of chimneys now available to them, swifts have used such other structures as empty wells and cisterns, out-buildings, silos, and barns. It is difficult to imagine that before the arrival of white men the chimney swift could possibly have been as numerous as it is today.

The nest is placed on the inside wall of a chimney, or hollow tree. It consists of small twigs glued together in the form of a half-cup which is cemented to the vertical surface. (The swift cannot take off from the ground, and it must collect nesting material while hovering on the wing.) The "glue" is the product of substances secreted by the bird's salivary glands, and is remarkably strong. Bird's nest soup is the end result of an even more highly refined practice among the cave swiftlets of the Far East, which build the entire nest of saliva. The "farthest out" swift nesting procedure I have seen is that of the palm swift of equatorial Africa, which glues its two eggs *on end* to a tiny patch of material cemented to a wildly swinging palm frond. If swifts could work out some method of incubating their eggs on the wing, no doubt they would soon be doing it.

Chimney swifts are solitary, not colonial, nesters, but in migration they are notably gregarious. Colossal flocks move together, roosting in suitable chimneys and such places, including trees, en route. John James Audubon tells of a giant hollow sycamore in which he estimated 9,000 swifts were roosting. Congregations between 5,000 and 10,000 have been reported in large chimneys. The greatest flock of birds I have ever seen consisted of swifts; in the Rift Valley of Kenya, Roger Tory Peterson and I could not begin to estimate the number of a great horde we watched one sundown – it could have been 100,000 birds, or even more. In this hemisphere, chimney swifts winter in the Amazon Basin – how many of them, no one knows.

This is the only swift in eastern North America; there are three others in the west, and about eighty species in the world.

Length 5¹/₂ inches.   Male, Overpeck Creek, New Jersey, June 5.

plate 37 — the sketch

RUBY-THROATED HUMMINGBIRD
Archilochus colubris

plate 37 RUBY-THROATED HUMMINGBIRD *Archilochus colubris*

THE smallest of all the higher vertebrates is a bird – the tiny bee hummingbird of Cuba – a mere 2¹/₄ inches long. The larger (for a hummingbird) ruby-throat is the only member of its family in eastern Canada, although others occur in the west. There are more than three hundred species of hummingbirds, all of them in the Americas, the majority in equatorial regions.

These are the only birds which habitually hover in mid-air, with a buzzy, insect-like wingbeat so rapid that the precise nature of it is impossible to see. We knew little about hummingbird flight before the arrival of high-speed photography, especially that done by Crawford H. Greenewalt, who likens a hummingbird to a helicopter in its technique. "To be sure, the wings go backward and forward, more like the oars of a boat than the circular whirl of the helicopter rotor. The effect, however, is much the same. If a helicopter hovers, the rotor is in a plane parallel to the earth's surface – so are the wings of a hummingbird. As the helicopter moves forward or backward, the rotor tilts in the appropriate direction – so do the wings of a hummingbird. The helicopter can rise directly from a given spot without a runway for take-off – so can a hummingbird."

Greenewalt's magnificent photographs brought to the world for the first time the almost unreal and unbelievable brilliance and beauty of this family of birds. Most of their blazing colours are the result of structural effects rather than pigmentation. The rather scaly feathers produce their iridescence from the play of light on their surfaces. The only true pigments in hummingbirds are black and rufous; all the rest of their gorgeous colours are mechanical. The result, in the words of Professor Jacques Berlioz, is "a brilliancy and a variety of tints unrivalled in any other group of birds."

As you might anticipate from their flamboyant appearance and volatile nature, male ruby-throated hummingbirds are confirmed philanderers, moving from partner to partner in the course of the breeding season. The female builds a nest by herself, and when she is ready to mate she does so, in a somewhat undiscriminating way, with the first male who comes along. He then departs in the search for other females, taking no part in the rearing of the brood. The nest is a delicate cup about 1¹/₂ inches wide, decorated with lichens and bound together by spider silk, firmly anchored across a suitably small branch. The two bean-sized eggs are white. Young birds are fed by regurgitation, on a fare that consists chiefly of flower nectar and diminutive insects. Feeding involves the most memorable sword-swallowing act ever chronicled. The parent stands over the young bird, and jams her long, sharp bill directly downward – and seemingly endlessly – into the young one's open gape. Demands for food are insatiable, and the old bird must work hard to satisfy them.

The fast-moving, almost perpetually airborne hummingbird uses up a great deal of energy. Hummingbirds have the highest metabolic rate of all vertebrates, even including that fiery mammalian furnace, the shrew. At sundown, when further foraging is impossible, the bird's metabolic processes must slow down and move at a more moderate rate for it to get through the night without starving. The bird thus slips into a semi-torpid condition which might, if extended for a period, lead towards true hibernation.

Length 3¹/₂ inches.   Male, Halifax, North Carolina, June 11. Female, Eastville, Va., June 18.

plate 38 — the sketch

BELTED KINGFISHER
Megaceryle alcyon

plate 38 BELTED KINGFISHER *Megaceryle alcyon*

KINGFISHERS are a cosmopolitan group of over eighty species, of which we have only one in Canada. Most kingfishers do not actually eat fish, and many live a long way from water of any kind. But all are highly predatory, and take insects, reptiles, and even small birds and mammals. The belted kingfisher is an inveterate fisherman, however, a special line of work which some authorities suggest may have developed after, not before, the group as a whole evolved. In other words, the spearlike bill may have been "pre-adapted" for fishing while the belted kingfisher was still chasing lizards and locusts like its relatives.

Except for its habit of plunging into the water after small fishes, the kingfisher is in no way an aquatic animal. Rather it behaves very much like its kin, the mot-mots, bee-eaters, and rollers, all of which perch motionless, flycatcher-like, on a branch or stub, waiting for some prey item (usually an invertebrate) to come by. It is easy to speculate that for the kingfishers, fishing is a recent development.

Kingfishers are solitary birds, with each pair demanding and defending a good stretch of riverside or lakeshore. They have favourite perches where they regularly sit to survey the water and its contents. They do not stick strictly to fish, however, and willingly take small crustaceans and insects, and some small mammals. The nest is situated at the end of a burrow about four or five feet long (sometimes as much as ten), which is dug into a vertical bank by the birds. The same tunnel may be used, and extended, year after year. Six or seven eggs are laid, and like those of so many hole-nesters, they are white. The young are in the nest for about a month.

On their first hunting excursions young kingfishers are awkward and clumsy; it takes time for them to reach a degree of proficiency. That the parents at least occasionally lend a helping hand in the learning process is clear in one report: an adult bird caught a fish, subdued it with a few whacks without actually killing it, then dropped it back into the water for one of the young birds to practice on.

The general rule among birds is that in those species where the sexes have different plumages, the male is the more colourful. The kingfisher is unconventional; it is the female who has the extra, chestnut "belt" from which the bird gets its name. In Canada, in addition to the kingfisher, only the phalaropes have this peculiarity, but in their case the male takes over all the duties of incubation. L. L. Snyder has evidence that this switch in kingfisher colour is accompanied by certain changes in the behavioural norm. He once saw "a mid-April courtship flight of a pair of belted kingfishers during which the female was the pursuer and the male the pursued."

Kingfishers are hardy birds; they arrive early in the spring and linger as long as they are able in the fall. Occasionally they over-winter in the most southerly parts of Canada, but most seem to move south to Florida, where they are particularly abundant. Along the Tamiami Trail in January there seems to be a kingfisher every few hundred feet – such proximity to their own species the birds would never tolerate at nesting time. Kingfishers breed from coast to coast, north as far as the Yukon, James Bay, and central Labrador.

Length 13 inches.   Female, Pierce, Idaho, July 1.

plate 39 — the sketch

YELLOW-SHAFTED FLICKER

Colaptes auratus

plate 39 YELLOW-SHAFTED FLICKER *Colaptes auratus*

THE flicker is our only woodpecker which (in the manner of the European green woodpecker) feeds much of the time on the ground. Other species do it very occasionally, but usually only in periods of acute food shortage. Flickers regularly probe our lawns and garden borders for ants and other small insects, although they are just as proficient at digging in trees as any other woodpeckers. Not many animals eat ants; the suggestion has been made that since the flicker habitually does, it proves that the bird has no sense of taste. On the other hand, zoo-keepers know that when the ant supply is low, South American giant ant-eaters can be induced to eat substitute food — even hamburger — so long as it is coated with formic acid. Surely it is possible, then, that flickers *can* taste, and that they *like* ants — and formic acid. They have unusually large salivary glands, which may have a function in neutralizing the acid.

Although they do so much foraging on the ground, flickers nest in trees like any other woodpeckers. Both sexes work at excavating a hole in a tree (usually a dead one) as high as 60 to 90 feet from the ground, although often much lower. Robie W. Tufts tells an interesting story about nesting. He put out a hollow stump as a nesting box for the birds, and placed sawdust in the bottom. Much to his surprise, as soon as they arrived in spring, "they began immediately to remove the sawdust, a beakful at a time, working in alternate shifts for the better part of two days." They then pecked off chunks of the log itself and let them fall to the bottom. That was, apparently, more to their taste.

The normal clutch is six to eight white eggs. Fourteen have been recorded, but that many could possibly be the product of two females. This is not to suggest, however, that flickers are incapable of laying unusual numbers of eggs. In one famous experiment, a flicker's eggs were removed from the nest as fast as they were laid, with the exception that one was always left as a "nest egg." In its attempt to cope with the daily loss of its labours, the bird laid 71 eggs in 73 days.

Another notable exercise involving flickers had to do with the ways in which the sexes recognize each other. Male flickers differ from females externally by the presence of a black "moustache" mark which the female lacks. The female of a pair was trapped, and artificial moustaches were stuck to her cheeks. When she was released, her mate immediately attacked her, taking her for an intruding strange male. When the moustaches were removed, he accepted her back immediately. Both sexes have a conspicuous white rump patch, which is especially prominent in flight. This is a more general recognition mark, narrowing the bird down to the species flicker; once that is determined, the facial markings identify the sex.

In southern British Columbia and the mountains of Alberta, this species is replaced by the very closely related red-shafted flicker, which also reaches into extreme south-western Saskatchewan. Hybrids between the two are common where their ranges overlap and, as you would expect, they appear orange. I have twice seen "orange-shafted flickers" at Rondeau Provincial Park on the north shore of Lake Erie, although the red-shafted does not normally occur in the east at all. Hybrids can be extremely variable in colour and pattern. In some, the colour in wings and tail is orange; in others, yellow and red feathers alternate, giving the *effect* of orange. The moustache marks of male hybrids may be either black or red — or they may even have one of each.

Yellow-shafted flickers are migratory, and although a few remain in southern parts during the winter, most spend the off-season in the central and southern United States. Except for the areas occupied by the red-shafted species, they are found in Canada from coast to coast, north to treeline.

Length 13 inches.   Male, Chester, South Carolina, October 1.

plate 41 — the sketch

RED-BELLIED WOODPECKER
Centurus carolinus

plate 41 ## RED-BELLIED WOODPECKER *Centurus carolinus*

THIS is an extremely local bird in Canada, breeding regularly only in south-western Ontario's Middlesex County, but it is typical of the great Carolinian hardwood forest, which has only limited representation in the area. It is also seen more or less regularly in the woodlands of Point Pelee National Park and Rondeau Provincial Park.

Although I had made some acquaintance with this attractive bird in the southern U.S., my first experience with it in Canada was an especially notable one. It had been learned from some source along the birders' grapevine that a farmer near Melbourne, Ontario, had found red-bellied woodpeckers nesting in his woodlot, and a carload of Toronto enthusiasts went to have a look. We arrived at the farmhouse, knocked on the door, and were told that the man we were looking for was out ploughing. In a field, we discovered a tractor busily snorting away, and perched somewhat incongruously on top was a very large man with binoculars slung round his neck and Peterson's *Field Guide* sticking from the pocket of dusty blue overalls. No more ploughing was done that day, as the jovial Dougal Murray showed us his woodpeckers. That was a good many years ago, and we all remember with affection our first introduction to a new (to us) Canadian nesting bird and the beginning of a long friendship. Skilled bird students pop up in some unexpected places.

This is the only Canadian woodpecker that combines a zebra-barred back with red on the head. Don't invest much time trying to see the red on the belly; it is there, in both sexes, but not readily discernible in the field. The bird has a churring call-note quite like that of the red-headed woodpecker, which often inhabits the same type of deciduous forest. It is quite noisy when feeding.

Unlike most woodpeckers, this species eats a good deal of vegetable food. Depending upon the season and the availability of forage, half of its diet may be made up of beech and acorn mast, berries and domestic fruit. It frequently stores food items such as acorns, nuts and insects for future use by jamming them into a crack in a post or tree trunk. In various parts of its range it is not above raiding corn cribs and orange groves. It often becomes quite tame and approachable.

Where they occur in winter, red-bellied woodpeckers come to feeding trays readily for suet, seeds, and dried fruit. They do not appear to migrate to any extent.

Length 9¹/₂ inches.   Male, Alexandra, Virginia, February 8.

plate 42 — the sketch

RED-HEADED WOODPECKER

Melanerpes erythrocephalus

plate 42 # RED-HEADED WOODPECKER *Melanerpes erythrocephalus*

SEVERAL of our woodpeckers are often wrongly identified as "red-headed" because they show some patch of red, but this one is the genuine article. It is undeniably one of the most handsome of North American birds. At rest, it is striking enough, but in flight, as it bares unexpectedly large snow-white wing patches in contrast with its blue-black body and blazing head, it is the most conspicuous bird we have.

Would that we had more of them. The red-head's fortunes have been intimately related to human activities, and it follows that they have been mixed. This is not a bird of the very deepest forest, so it is possible that in pioneer times it was not especially abundant. Then, with the clearing of the land, it became a relatively common bird at the edges of fields, in open forests and untidy orchards. A bit later, two new factors sent its numbers into a sharp decline. The first was the advent of "clean farming," which involved the taking out of dead or dying orchard trees, the removal of deadwood from farm woodlots, the replacement of old, rotten fenceposts, and the general tidying up of the land. The hole-nesting birds were in immediate trouble.

The widespread clean-up was one problem; another was new and formidable competition for the few sites that remained. The European starling, introduced to this continent at New York City in 1890, also nests in holes. It spread with astonishing speed. The red-headed woodpecker is a strong and vigorous bird, but in most places it was no match for the incredibly adaptable and successful starling. The foreign intruder also routed the similarly vulnerable eastern bluebird.

A new and completely unanticipated hazard appeared with the automobile. The red-headed woodpecker has the unfortunate habit of perching on fence-posts, then taking off in a low dip across the road. A great many are killed by passing cars — a mortality factor that no one could have guessed at two generations ago.

Now, however, I think that the bird's chances may be improving slightly — at least for the moment. Nothing ever seems to happen in nature without someone deriving some good from it somehow, and perhaps now it is the turn of this singularly hard-pressed woodpecker. In the last several years, the imported fungus infection called Dutch elm disease has taken a terrible toll of trees in eastern Canada. Its spread has been largely unchecked for perfectly understandable economic reasons. The disease is transmitted by bark beetles which transfer it from dead wood to living trees. Dead elms are thus reservoirs of the infection, and should be removed. But they are very costly to remove, and a great many more remain standing than have been taken care of in "sanitation" campaigns. These standing dead elms are beginning, in my view, to contribute to a modest recovery of the red-headed woodpecker (and, just possibly, of the eastern bluebird).

Dead wood provides both nesting sites and a supply of wood-boring insects and other animal food. But the red-head is not limited to the diet afforded by dead trees. It readily eats fruits, berries, and nuts. It also engages with surprising success in the unwoodpecker-like practice of flycatching — chasing and snapping up winged insects in mid-air. It is also occasionally alleged to take the eggs and young of other birds, and has even been known to attack a mouse. It is a remarkably versatile and flexible bird, if only we will give it a chance in the form of breeding sites.

Length 9³/₄ inches.   Male, Colorado.

plate 43 — the sketch

DOWNY WOODPECKER
Dendrocopos pubescens

plate 43

DOWNY WOODPECKER *Dendrocopos pubescens*

OUR smallest woodpecker is also one of the most generally and intimately known. It readily visits backyard feeding stations in winter, and nests in pretty well all parts of the country north to the limit of trees. The similar but larger hairy woodpecker breeds over much the same area. The simplest way to distinguish the two is by their bills: the hairy's bill is large, almost as long as its head; the downy's is very short and stubby, much smaller than the length of its head. As is so often the case, our birds of the genus *Dendrocopos* have their Old World counterparts in the three species of European spotted woodpeckers. Others occur in Africa and Asia. There is a wonderful and varied proliferation of woodpeckers in the world – more than two hundred species of them. They range in size from tiny birds less than four inches long to striking giants almost as large as a raven. Many of them have at least some red about the head, but as we have seen, there is only one redheaded woodpecker.

Woodpeckers are finely specialized for their unique way of life. Since most of them live on the insects that infest the rotting bark of diseased and dead trees, they have developed appropriate structural adaptations. Usually insects have to be dug out, so the bill is long, strong, and chisel-like. It is mounted on an unusually large and heavy skull, and driven by a flexible and slender but very strong neck. The tongue of a woodpecker is extraordinarily long; it can be extended deep into an insect gallery. Its tip is often armed with spear-points, barbs, or bristles, as with the sapsuckers, depending upon the specialty of that particular species.

Since most of the time they are working vertically, parallel to the tree trunk, woodpeckers prop themselves against it by means of unusually stiff tail feathers. Strong feet hold the bird firmly to the bark as it chips away. The feet are built for clinging, and not many woodpeckers go in for proper perching on twigs or branches. The little downy is an exception to this rule; it commonly forages in smaller bushes and shrubs, and frequently perches crosswise in the manner typical of songbirds, but one that is uncharacteristic of woodpeckers.

Most of our woodpeckers do not migrate to any great extent, but populations seem to shift southward in the autumn, withdrawing from the more extreme regions of their range. We have downy woodpeckers with us all year long, but they may or may not be the same individuals in both summer and winter. In the most southern areas, they are probably sedentary, year-round residents. Downy woodpeckers are especially noticeable in the spring, when their courtship involves much noisy chasing about, high-pitched chattering, and rapid drumming on some suitable sounding-board.

The nest is dug by both sexes in a branch or trunk that is often softened by disease and insects to allow easy access, although they will sometimes dig successfully in sound wood. An average of five eggs is laid in the chips at the bottom of the cavity; they make no conventional nest. Both parents take care of the young birds, which emerge from the nesting hole and climb about on the trees before they can actually fly.

Length 6 inches.   *Male, Louisville, Georgia, December 27.*
Female, Fort Thompson, Florida, February 28.

plate 44 — the sketch

EASTERN KINGBIRD

Tyrannus tyrannus

plate 44 ## EASTERN KINGBIRD *Tyrannus tyrannus*

EW summer birds are as noisily conspicuous as this one. Intemperate, belligerent, a kingbird can hardly escape the notice of anyone with or without an interest in birds. Far from being shy and self-obliterating, as so many birds are, it seems to call attention to itself in every conceivable way.

Many of the larger flycatchers are pugnacious animals, but the kingbird in particular does not hesitate to assault any large bird that comes into its area. As Earl Godfrey has put it, "A crow, hawk, heron or other large bird passing nearby is immediately and ignominiously driven off by the fury and agility of the kingbird's attack." Kingbirds have been known to fly at vultures, people, and – on at least one occasion – a low-flying small aircraft.

The tyrant flycatchers are a New World family, mostly tropical, comprising some 365 species, of which 22 are on the Canadian list. Many of them have strident voices; none could be called a "singer." To feed, a flycatcher typically perches on some eminence that commands a good unobstructed view of the area. When a flying insect is sighted, the bird launches itself in a fluttering swoop, snaps up the morsel, and sails back to its perch. The kingbird is especially distinguished for the arrogant, cavalier way in which it does it. Calling loudly whether perched or flying, grandly fanning its white-tipped black tail, the vociferous bird defiantly presides over his feeding territory.

Concealed in the black feathers of its crown the kingbird has a brilliant orange-red patch which is said to be displayed in moments of high agitation. When you consider that this species appears to be in a chronic state of agitation, it is surprising that the crown patch is so infrequently seen. There are reports of its being used in display between competing males, and for the intimidation of potential enemies, but I have only rarely and fleetingly seen it in the field.

The kingbird is flexible in its choice of nesting sites. Usually the bulky, well lined nest is built from ten to twenty feet up in a tree (normally in the open), or in shrubs adjoining watercourses. William Smith showed me one nest which was in the top of a stump in a quiet bay, scarcely a foot above the surrounding water. The usual four eggs are considered by some people to be the most beautiful in all the world of birds – creamy white, spotted with a variety of combinations of different colors.

Kingbirds are like all flycatchers in their absolute dependence on hatches of flying insects for their livelihood. Their seasonal activities are therefore governed by the temperature, and they are forced to be conscientious migrants. Although they are very jealous of territorial prerogatives at nesting time, they are notably gregarious during migration. One of the best places to see masses of kingbirds, whether in spring or fall, is Point Pelee National Park. The tip of the point is often alive with dozens of kingbirds – sometimes hundreds – all moving about with their stiff, "tip-of-the-wings" flight, all calling shrilly. On some occasions in the spring, the northward-moving birds are unfortunate enough to encounter a sharp drop in temperature, which eliminates all flying insects for a day or two. Then, it is possible to see kingbirds foraging on the sandy beaches or in the grass for alternative invertebrates. They will also take wild fruits when pressed.

Length 8¹/₂ inches.   Male, St. Paul, Minnesota, June 21.

plate 45 — the sketch

GREAT CRESTED FLYCATCHER
Myiarchus crinitus

plate 45 ## GREAT CRESTED FLYCATCHER *Myiarchus crinitus*

THIS showy flycatcher provides much of the colour – for eye and ear – in our southern woodlands. It is a good-sized bird for one of its family, with a full-throated, harsh, and carrying voice. Few people can have failed to hear its ringing *weep!* even though they may not have known the source. When the bird is glimpsed as it flourishes after an insect in the dense canopy of the forest, its cinnamon-rufous tail is the best field mark.

There are several other quite similar members of the genus *Myiarchus*, three in the United States and more in Central and South America (there is even one in the far-off Galapagos archipelago), but Canada has only this one. All are much the same in general appearance and behaviour. This proliferation of the genus reflects the wide spectrum of food possibilities that is available in the warmer regions. The closer you move to the equator, the greater the amount and variety of insect life, and the wider the opportunities for specialization and thus radiation among closely-related and presumably recently evolved birds.

The crested flycatcher nests in holes, and its environment being what it is, it frequently uses the abandoned cavities of woodpeckers. Natural holes are used as well, and occasionally the birds will condescend to nest in an artificial box. The nest itself is very interesting, often resembling a kind of trash-heap more than it does a bird's nest. Some surprising materials and objects somehow find their way into the crested flycatcher's home. A. C. Bent has listed some of them: leaves, animal hair, chicken and other poultry feathers, bark fibres from trees, hemp, rootlets, pieces of cord string, strands from ropes, large quantities of grass and pine needles, a few small twigs, feathers of grouse, owls, and hawks, a rabbit's tail, woodchuck fur, seed pods, bits of bark, cloth, and paper, pieces of onion skin, cellophane, paraffined or oiled paper, bits of eggshells, and pieces of horse manure.

But of all the improbable things that are found in the nests of crested flycatchers, the one that has puzzled ornithologists the most is the occasional presence of cast-off snakeskin. This raises a difficult question. What in the world could be its function? No one really knows, but since there is some similarity between dry snakeskin and some of the other favoured materials – onion skin, wax paper, cellophane, and so on – the bird would seem to be attracted by the texture and perhaps the shininess and even the noisiness of the material. But as Lester Snyder says in *Ontario Birds*, "We cannot attribute a purpose in respect to such habits of birds, and often, as in the present instance, it is not always possible to perceive that the species derives any special benefit from certain fixed habits." In other words, there doesn't always have to be a reason for everything.

In Canada, the great crested flycatcher breeds in suitable leafy forests from south-eastern Saskatchewan through southern Ontario to the lower half of New Brunswick, straggling into Nova Scotia.

Length 9 inches.   Male, La Raya, Rio Cauca, Bolivar, Colombia, January 22.

plate 46 — the sketch

EASTERN PHOEBE
Sayornis phoebe

plate 46 EASTERN PHOEBE *Sayornis phoebe*

We all have our pet "gripes," and one of mine has always been the name of this bird. To my ear, the bird does not say the word *phoebe* nearly as clearly as, for example, the black-capped chickadee does, or, for that matter, the eastern wood pewee. This can be misleading to beginners, but tradition and usage are such that we seem to be stuck with it. The phoebe's voice is harsh and raspy; the chickadee and pewee whistle the two-syllable song.

The phoebe is dignified historically as the very first species of bird to be banded or ringed in North America. The imaginative experiment was conducted by the great John James Audubon, when he lived at Mill Grove, in Pennsylvania. He attached light threads to the legs of nestling phoebes (just to complicate the issue, he called them "peewees"), but found that they invariably removed them. "I renewed them, however, until I found the little fellows habituated to them; and at last, when they were about to leave the nest, I fixed a light silver thread to the leg of each, loose enough not to hurt the part, but so fashioned that no effort of theirs could remove it." Next spring, when the birds returned to the area, Audubon "had the pleasure of finding two of them had the little ring on the leg."

Audubon did not have to wait long for the birds to return, as phoebes are among the very first migrants to turn up after the winter — much the earliest of the flycatchers. At that time of year, when there may or may not be a sufficient supply of midges and other flying insects, phoebes frequently resort to vegetable food. I have seen them eating the white berries of poison ivy in such circumstances.

Phoebes have a special affinity for water, and also for man-made structures. The happy combination of the two in the form of small bridges is the most usual place in which to find a mud-and-greenstuff cup nest which is securely fastened to a beam or trestle. Other structures are used, such as cottages, barns, and out-buildings, where ledges and eaves offer shelter. Before there were such things to nest on, the birds liked to use rocky ledges with some overhang above them, but such sites were hard to come by.

The phoebe is a plain little bird, but an appealing one. There are several superficially similar small flycatchers; the phoebe is separated from the others instantly by its habit of flirting its tail up and down. You could not really call it "wagging" because it is usually in a more or less vertical plane, but it is an absolutely diagnostic feature. This bird has no other conspicuous field characteristics; the others have various combinations of eye-rings and wing-bars, both of which the adult phoebe lacks. The phoebe's bill is black — a useful mark at close range. At a distance, the entire large head appears black, in contrast to the dusky look of the back.

The eastern phoebe ranges in Canada from New Brunswick west and north to the Mackenzie, east of the Rocky Mountains. The related Say's phoebe, a somewhat more handsome, pale bird with a black tail and rusty-cinnamon underparts, is a westerner that does not often venture farther east than the Saskatchewan-Manitoba border, although wanderers have turned up in Ontario and Quebec.

Length 7 inches.   Male, Overpeck Creek, New Jersey, September 11.

plate 47 — the sketch

EASTERN WOOD PEWEE

Contopus virens

plate 47   # EASTERN WOOD PEWEE *Contopus virens*

SOME of our smaller flycatchers can be quite bewildering in the field, especially the very smallest ones, the members of the genus *Empidonax*. They are all more or less greenish in colour, with wing-bars and eye-rings. The wood pewee, on the other hand, is an essentially grey bird, with wing-bars but *no* eye-ring. The wing-bars and the pale lower mandible separate it from the slightly larger phoebe. But the two are rarely seen together. The phoebe is a very early migrant, arriving in early to mid-April, while the more sluggish pewee is not expected until about the third week in May. The phoebe frequents human buildings; the pewee prefers the shady retreat of hardwood forests.

Many birds are already well along with nesting by the time the pewees come on the scene. You are not likely to see them arrive; the first clue to their presence is generally the slow, plaintive *pee-a-wee* that seems to float down lazily and reluctantly from the green canopy above. There is a reason for the pewee's late arrival in spring. It is not so likely to eat vegetable food as the phoebe is; since it is almost entirely dependent on insects, its slow progress northward is a form of insurance against a late spring and possible thin times on the way to its breeding grounds.

The pewee hunts as most flycatchers do, by waiting on a favourite perch until a desirable insect flies by. Unlike the phoebe and kingbird, however, which hunt in the open, the pewee chooses a dead branch or twig somewhere up in the broad-leaved foliage, and works from there. It darts out with a quick flutter, takes up an insect with its sturdy, flattened bill (sometimes aided by the stiff bristles which surround its mouth) – often with an audible sharp *snap*. It may take more than one victim before swinging round and back to its perch again. Most of these prey items are very small flies and bees, but A. Dawes Dubois saw an adult pewee return to the nest "with a good-sized butterfly, a red admiral, which the young bird swallowed, wings and all."

The surprisingly small nest of the wood pewee is saddled across a horizontal branch, decorated with lichens. Generally it is from twenty to forty feet up. Usually, there are three eggs; they are creamy-white with an arrangement of variously coloured blotches and spots around the larger end. Incubation takes slightly under two weeks, and the young birds soon appear to be much too large for a nest that was none too roomy for the sitting adult in the first place. Young songbirds grow rapidly; the pewees are ready to leave the nest in about fifteen to eighteen days.

It is a short summer. The wood pewees nested some time in June, and a few weeks later they are ready for fall migration. They leave earlier than most, but they are leisurely little birds, and they have a long way to go. Flying by night, they make their way to Central and South America.

The eastern wood pewee nests from south-eastern Manitoba through southern Ontario and Quebec to the Maritimes. Its counterpart in the rest of the country is the western wood pewee, which breeds from the southern part of the Yukon and the Mackenzie through the entire western area to south-central Manitoba. The two species (surely they cannot have been separate species for very long) are almost indistinguishable in the field except for their voices. The western wood pewee has a harsh and nasal song in contrast to the clear, whistled notes of the eastern bird.

Length 6¹/₂ inches.   Male, Glenwood, Illinois, May 26.

plate 48 — the sketch

TREE SWALLOW
Iridoprocne bicolor

plate 48   # TREE SWALLOW *Iridoprocne bicolor*

*T*HE brilliant metallic-blue lustre of the male tree swallow is one of the great pleasures of early springtime. On the average, the birds arrive soon after the middle of April. That is an early date for an insectivorous bird, a gamble on an early hatch of small flying insects sufficient to carry them through. But it is not all left to chance. The more northern populations of tree swallows are in part vegetarian. They are known to be fond of bayberries, which can sustain them in weather that discourages tiny invertebrates. But tree swallows of the south are not so versatile; they are totally insectivorous, which means that in cold snaps and resulting insect famine they are more vulnerable than their northern counterparts.

I have seen tree swallows darting about the stiff, naked branches of a flooded wood while there was still much ice and snow, and only patches of open water. What they were feeding on was not evident. These are tough birds, however, and when the very first tentative, warming rays of sunshine release hordes of midges, their summer has begun.

In the days before settlement, tree swallows nested — as most of them still do — in holes in trees, preferably near water. But many of them have now taken to artificial nesting boxes, where they are available. Eastern bluebirds prefer boxes of the same size and type, and this has occasionally led to trouble.

In A. C. Bent's *Life Histories*, F. Seymour Hersey gives an account of a dispute between the two species. Bluebirds were already occupying a nesting box in his garden, when a pair of tree swallows arrived and gave signs that they wanted that box.

Mr. Hersey promptly put up two more boxes, but the swallows ignored them and persisted in attempting to evict the bluebirds (which already had eggs). This they finally accomplished, and the bluebirds moved into one of the new boxes, leaving the tree swallows in occupation of the first. Then a second pair of tree swallows appeared, and drove the unfortunate bluebirds away for good.

The fortunes of this kind of competition can go either way, however. William H. Carrick, the renowned naturalist-cameraman, witnessed a similar encounter when he was living in Uxbridge, Ontario. He had placed out bird boxes, one of which was occupied by a pair of tree swallows. In this instance, bluebirds invaded the box at one of those rare times when both of the tree swallows were absent, threw out the three swallow eggs, and took over. It is doubtful whether this would have been the outcome had one of the swallows been present. It would seem that tree swallows and bluebirds are reasonably evenly matched, but like the red-headed woodpecker, both have suffered grievously from competition with the hole-nesting European starling.

Tree swallows have an interesting and delightful habit of using white feathers, where they are available, for lining their nests. These are in good supply around most chicken-yards, but in areas where they are scarce they seem to be a very desirable commodity, keenly contended for. Once it has got one, a bird will occasionally play with a white feather, catching and releasing it in the air and doing all sorts of complex aerobatics in the process — a charming sight.

Length 6 inches.   Male, Benemah Co. St. Maries, Idaho, April 1.

plate 49 — the sketch

BANK SWALLOW

Riparia riparia

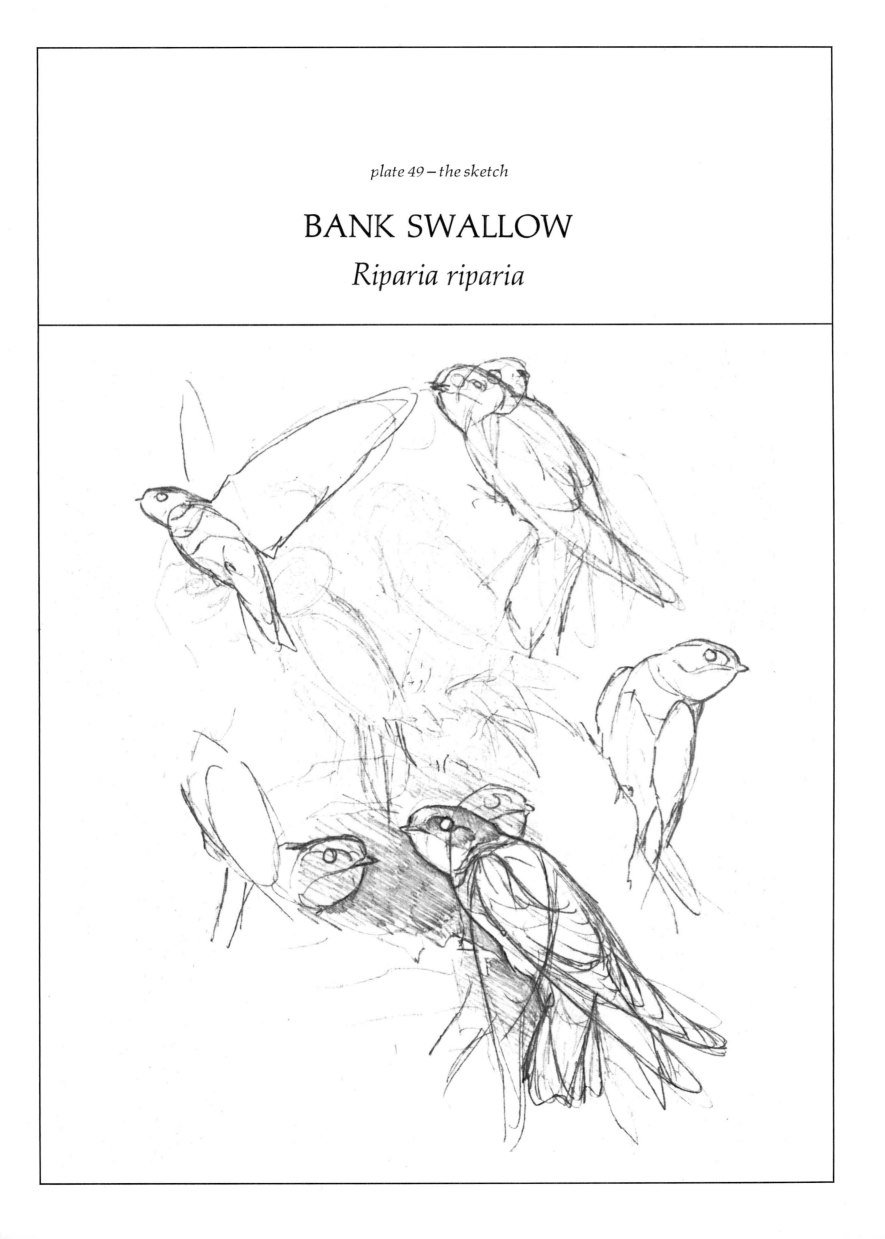

plate 49 ## BANK SWALLOW *Riparia riparia*

Our smallest, most delicate swallow is known as the sand martin in Britain; the two populations are of the same species. Both its colloquial and scientific names accurately describe the bird's best-known characteristic: it nests in burrows dug into the vertical sides of the banks of streams and lakes. You will also find its colonies in the sides of quarries, gravel pits, and other human excavations, including road and railway cuts. It is the only swallow to habitually do this, although it is the regular practice among some kingfishers; mot-mots, bee-eaters, and the like.

It is mysterious how a slight, fragile-looking little bird like a swallow, with its tiny bill and feet, can burrow from two to four feet, or even more, into the earth. Dayton Stoner has described the process in A. C. Bent's *Life Histories*. Both sexes take part in the digging, which is accomplished with much jabbing by the beak, scratching with the feet, and a sort of "shuffling" movement of the wings which apparently helps the bird to get rid of loose dirt.

At the end of the tunnel there is a feather-lined nest in which is laid an average of five white eggs. They are incubated, and the young brooded and fed, by both parents. The young are in the nest for about three weeks before reaching the flight stage, but are said to return to the burrow for the night during the first month. A young bird reared in a tunnel would seemingly have little chance to exercise its wings and none to practice flying – a limitation, one would think, for a bird so aerial as a swallow. Its first aerial venture has to be successful – and usually is. Depending on the location of a colony and the prevailing weather, a second brood may be raised in the course of the summer.

The bank swallow breeds from coast to coast roughly to the limit of trees from the Yukon to Labrador, with the exception of south-western British Columbia and the eastern three-quarters of Newfoundland. It winters in South America; in the Old World, in Africa and southern Asia. For years, people could not explain its sudden disappearance each fall. Its migrations – or, more properly, its absence in winter – led to the legend (from Aristotle and Pliny the Elder onward) that the swallow was a hibernator. Its strange habit of living in colonies in holes tunnelled into the ground must have helped give rise to the legend. No less a pundit than Dr. Samuel Johnson informed us that swifts, swallows, and others "conglobulated" in a ball and spent the winter asleep in the mud at the bottom of frozen ponds. Many people believed that swallows and other birds flew to the moon to spend the winter. (Now that a hibernating bird *(Plate 35) has* been found, however, perhaps we will have to review the literature with more humility.)

It is interesting that the bank swallow exhibits somewhat loose family ties. Although both sexes may look after the eggs and hatchlings, the female is known to leave the brood to the sole attention of the male parent, while she seeks out a different partner for the second brood of the summer. This laxity in the pair bond is unusual among small birds, but it does occur also in the house wren, while hummingbirds *(Plate 37)* reach the height of promiscuity. Young bank swallows are ready to breed when they are less than one year old, that is, at the beginning of the spring following the summer in which they were hatched.

Length 5¹/₄ inches. *Female, Lewiston, Idaho, September 1.*

plate 50 — the sketch

ROUGH-WINGED SWALLOW

Stelgidopteryx ruficollis

plate 50 ROUGH-WINGED SWALLOW *Stelgidopteryx ruficollis*

Sᴏᴍᴇ bird names are of considerable value in field recognition; others are not. This is one of the latter. The name is derived from an anatomical peculiarity that is only evident visually under magnification. But if you stroke the outer edge of the outermost flight feather, you will feel a certain roughness which is caused by hundreds of tiny hooks along its edge; their function is not known. Either way, you have to have the bird in the hand.

This is the most southern of our swallows; although it breeds from British Columbia to the south-western corner of Quebec, it is confined to a very narrow band that in some areas is just a few miles north of the border of the U.S. It is much more common and widely distributed to the south of us — all the way to southern Brazil. Identification is a matter of separating it from our only other brown-backed species, the bank swallow. That bird is smaller, has a conspicuous dark breast-band, and a much more erratic, irregular flight. The larger rough-wing has a dull wash on the throat, and flies more directly, with fewer wingbeats.

In the manner of a bank swallow, this species occasionally burrows into sand banks and other exposed surfaces to build its nest. But unlike the bank swallow, it is not colonial, and will nest in any suitable crevice or cranny in a rock face, or even on a human structure of some kind. It is very adaptable in this sense, but its solitary nesting habits no doubt tend to keep its numbers down.

Joseph Grinnell and T. I. Storer in *Animal Life in the Yosemite* described the attractive courtship flight of the rough-winged swallow. "From time to time the males were seen in pursuit of the females and, while so engaged, to make rather striking use of their seemingly plain garb. They would spread the long white feathers at the lower base of the tail until they curled up along either side of the otherwise brownish tail. The effect produced was of white outer tail feathers, such as those of the junco or pipit. Males can by means of this trick be distinguished from the females at a distance of fully fifty yards."

John James Audubon was the discoverer of the rough-winged swallow. He first noticed a flock of the birds when he was living at Bayou Sara, in Louisiana. They looked so much like bank swallows that he nearly overlooked them, but something prompted him to collect four or five of them. He looked at them, "thought them rather large," and popped them in his bag for further examination at leisure. A number of years later, his friend Rev. John Bachman, of Charleston, S.C., sent him four swallows' eggs which he said were laid by birds that looked very much like bank swallows, but which nested in the walls of an unfinished brick house. Bachman said. "It is now believed that there are two species of these birds." Indeed there were, and on his next trip to Charleston, Audubon collected a pair which were the basis for his scientific description.

I have seen this species in November and December in Guatemala, but at that season would have no way of knowing whether the birds were from our part of the world or were local and non-migratory. This points up one of the weaknesses of bird study based on field observation alone. Banding is one of the obvious answers to this problem. But we should never overlook the vital importance of adequate study collections; only a specimen in the hand, in the lack of a banding record, could have answered my Central American question.

Length 5³/₄ inches.   Male, Mississippi, September 27.

plate 51 — the sketch

CLIFF SWALLOW
Petrochelidon pyrrhonota

plate 51

CLIFF SWALLOW *Petrochelidon pyrrhonota*

EW birds are as legendary as this one. Though only one legend surrounds it, that one is enough, for this is the famous swallow of the mission of San Juan Capistrano, in California. Widely publicized for their allegedly unchangeable arrival time at the mission each spring, the birds were even the subject of a popular song I vaguely remember from the thirties. Jim Baillie has the secret. "The swallows always turn up on the same day because no one would dare look for them *before* March 19." The same phenomenon existed at one time in Toronto, where the whimbrels always used to arrive on May 24. They don't any longer – probably because the holiday date has been changed. They now arrive on the Monday *nearest* to May 24 – an extraordinary development which perhaps deserves further study.

Even if the Capistrano myth has been exploded, it in no way detracts from the cliff swallow's fame as a migrant. It nests as far north as Alaska, and winters from Brazil to Argentina. We usually think of a swallow as a slight, darting, buoyantly flying little bird; we rarely think of the enormous challenge it faces twice each year on its migratory journeys.

In the mid-1930s, Frederick C. Lincoln plotted on a map the average spring arrival dates of the cliff swallow. By linking the spots at which birds arrived on certain dates, he came up with isochronal lines which shed much light on the nature of the swallow's migratory progress. On March 10 western migrants are at the top of the Gulf of California; eastern birds are still as far south as Mexico City. By March 30, birds travelling up the west coast have almost reached Vancouver, whereas those in the east are still on the Gulf coast of Texas. By the middle of June both Alaskan and Maritime birds have reached their final nesting grounds.

Why this slow-down by eastern birds around the Gulf of Mexico? It is a detour that adds at least 2,000 miles to the trip. Why do the birds not fly across rather than around the Gulf? Lincoln reasoned that the cliff swallow is a daytime migrant, and that, unlike many birds, it feeds throughout its journey. As he points out, "Flying along the insect-teeming shores of the Gulf of Mexico, the 2,000 extra miles that are added to its migration route are but a fraction of the distance that these birds actually cover in pursuit of their food." Anyone who has watched a cliff swallow fluttering after insects like a bat will see the point of the argument.

Cliff swallows might more properly be called "eave swallows," because even though many of them still nest on cliffs, many more use the eaves of houses, cottages, barns, and out-buildings. The nest is intriguing from an engineering point of view. It resembles superficially a small flask, or bee-hive, built of little mud or clay pellets which are gathered in appropriately moist locations and cemented together. There is usually a protruding, retort-like neck which is used as entrance and exit, but sometimes the nest is not roofed over, and somewhat resembles that of a barn swallow.

The fate of the nest and its occupants is often predetermined by the materials used, and their quality varies from place to place. Naturally clay is the best and strongest substance. Nests built too hastily or in very damp weather sometimes collapse before they are finished; others dry out, become crumbly, and may be the victims of summer thundershowers. In many parts of its range, the cliff swallow has been gradually edged out by competition from the imported house sparrow, whose liking for farm buildings is well known.

Length 6 inches.   *Lac la Hache, British Columbia, May 19.*

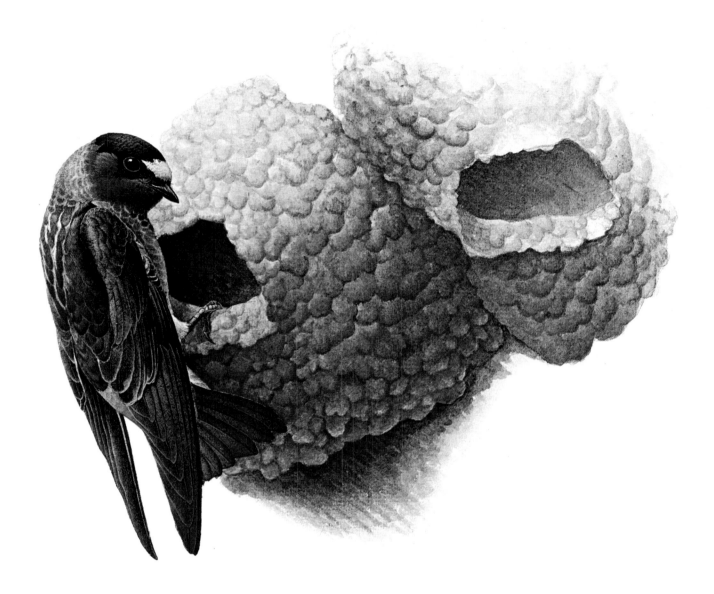

plate 52 — the sketch

PURPLE MARTIN

Progne subis

plate 52 ## PURPLE MARTIN *Progne subis*

LTHOUGH it is by no means the most common, our largest swallow is probably held in more affectionate regard than any other bird – and often by people who scarcely know another species. The reason is the martin's willingness to forsake hollow trees for its colonial nesting and to use man-made bird houses. Often these are "high rise" apartment buildings with twenty or even two hundred compartments. Martins do not appear to mind how ornate these structures become; many I have seen are so baroque that you would expect them to frighten the birds away for good. The boxes are placed on poles up to about twenty feet in the air, and a circular metal squirrel guard is often a good idea.

Martins are unpredictable birds, however, and seem to be choosy about the boxes they will occupy. One house may be overflowing while another nearby is completely ignored; the reason is rarely apparent. Sometimes it will take several years before they will accept a new box, but once they do, they will return year after year.

In Bent's *Life Histories*, Alexander Sprunt Jr. tells a remarkable story of the purple martin's homing instinct. "One of the most striking examples of a returning martin colony I ever heard was related to me by Alston Clapp, of Houston, Texas. While in his yard on one occasion he showed me his colony and said that the year previous he had taken down the house to paint it. Something delayed him, and it was not up when the martins arrived. Attracted by a great chattering one morning, he went out into the garden and saw the birds fluttering and circling about in the air *where the house should have been,* at the exact elevation occupied by it when placed!"

In spring, the martins arrive in our latitudes about the beginning of May. Unfortunately, the introduced house sparrow and starling begin nesting earlier than that, and many of the choicest sites are already occupied when the martins get here. This has had a serious effect on martin populations in many places. Many people who keep bird houses get around the problem by leaving the entrance holes boarded up until the first martins arrive. From that point on, they can generally look after themselves.

Like other swallows, the purple martin lives almost exclusively on flying invertebrates – winged insects, drifting young spiders, and the like, although the bird is also known sometimes to exhibit a great (and inexplicable) fondness for egg-shells. Almost all of its food is caught on the wing, and it drinks while in flight by dipping its bill into the water, as other swallows, and swifts, do. Audubon noted that martins even bathe while on the wing, "when over a large lake or river, giving a sudden motion to the hind part of the body, as it comes into contact with the water, thus dipping themselves into it, and then rising and shaking their body, like a water spaniel, to throw off the water."

Considering that the purple martin has been a familiar dooryard bird since the first white settlements in North America, and that even the Indians were on friendly terms with it, it is unusual that nothing whatever was known of its winter range until quite recently. Each fall, the birds simply disappeared off the face of the earth. The advent of widespread bird-banding cleared up the mystery. In 1936, a bird banded in Minnesota was found in Para, Brazil. It is now thought that almost the entire North American population winters in the Amazon Basin. Since its nearest relatives are all tropical or sub-tropical species, no doubt the purple martin is a northward pioneer of a sort, and its dramatic return to equatorial regions for the winter sheds light on the evolution of traditional migratory behaviour.

*Length 8 inches.   Male, May 9.
Female, Laurel, Maryland, September 13.*

Bibliography and Index

Bibliography

The birdwatcher is blessed with an extremely wide range of reading —
from books especially for the beginner to the vast advanced literature
of ornithology. The selection of titles presented here does not pretend
to be more than a sample of the sources available; it is offered merely as
an introduction to the subject, and includes both elementary and more
advanced references. It represents chiefly those sources most frequently
consulted by the author over the years. Many of them contain substantial bibliographies.

Identification

PETERSON, ROGER TORY, *A Field Guide to the Birds*. Boston: Houghton
Mifflin, 1947.

POUGH, RICHARD H., *Audubon Land Bird Guide*. Garden City: Doubleday, 1946. *Audubon Water Bird Guide*. Garden City: Doubleday, 1951.

ROBBINS, CHANDLER S., BRUNN, BERTEL, and ZIM, HERBERT S., *illustrated by*
ARTHUR SINGER, *Birds of North America*. New York: Golden Press, 1966.

*These books are visual aids to bird identification. In many cases, how-
ever, the song or call note of a bird may serve as corroboration of a
sighting, and occasionally may be even more important than the appearance of a bird. A number of long-play bird recordings of excellent
quality has appeared in recent years, and the number is growing. Some
are collections of birds of geographic regions; others contain families of
birds. For details, the reader is referred to the Federation of Ontario
Naturalists, Don Mills, Ontario, Canada.*

General and Reference

AMERICAN ORNITHOLOGISTS' UNION, *Check-list of North American Birds*
(5th edition). Baltimore: A.O.U., 1957.

AUSTIN, OLIVER L. JR., *and* SINGER, ARTHUR, *Birds of the World*. New York:
Golden Press, 1961.

BENT, ARTHUR C., *Life Histories of North American Birds* (20 vols.).
Washington: United States National Museum, 1919-1958.

BERGER, ANDREW J., *Bird Study*. New York: J. Wiley and Sons, 1961.

CRUICKSHANK, ALLAN *and* HELEN, *1001 Questions Answered About Birds*.
New York: Dodd, Mead, 1958.

DARLING, LOIS *and* LOUIS, *Bird*. Boston: Houghton Mifflin, 1962.

DORST, JEAN, *The Migrations of Birds*. Boston: Houghton Mifflin, 1963.

FISHER, JAMES, *and* PETERSON, ROGER TORY, *The World of Birds*. Garden
City: Doubleday, 1963.

FORBUSH, E. H., *and* MAY, JOHN B., *A Natural History of the Birds of
Eastern and Central North America*. Boston: Houghton Mifflin, 1939.

HALL, HENRY MARION, *edited by* ROLAND C. CLEMENT, *A Gathering of Shore
Birds*. New York: Devin Adair, 1960.

HICKEY, J. J., *A Guide to Bird Watching*. New York: Oxford University
Press, 1943.

KORTRIGHT, F. H., *Ducks, Geese and Swans of North America*. Washington: American Wildlife Institute, 1942.

PALMER, RALPH S. (ed.), *Handbook of North American Birds* (Vol. 1). New Haven: Yale University Press, 1962.

PETERSON, ROGER TORY, *The Bird Watcher's Anthology* (ed.), New York: Harcourt, Brace, 1957. *Birds Over America*. New York: Dodd, Mead, 1964.

PETERSON, ROGER TORY *and* THE EDITORS OF LIFE, *The Birds*. New York: Time Inc., 1963.

PETTINGILL, OLIN SEWALL JR., *A Guide to Bird Finding (East)*. New York: Oxford University Press, 1951. (ed.), *The Bird Watcher's America*. New York: McGraw-Hill, 1965.

THOMSON, A. LANDSBOROUGH (ed.), *A New Dictionary of Birds*. London: Nelson, 1964.

VAN TYNE, JOSSELYN, *and* BERGER, ANDREW J., *Fundamentals of Ornithology*. New York: J. Wiley and Sons, 1959.

WELTY, JOEL CARL, *The Life of Birds*. New York: Alfred A. Knopf, 1963.

Canadian

GODFREY, W. EARL, *The Birds of Canada*. Ottawa: National Museum of Canada Bulletin No. 203, 1966.

LIVINGSTON, JOHN A., *illustrated by* J. FENWICK LANSDOWNE, *Birds of the Northern Forest*. Toronto: McClelland and Stewart; Boston: Houghton Mifflin, 1966.

MUNRO, J. A., *and* COWAN, IAN MCTAGGART, *A Review of the Bird Fauna of British Columbia*. Victoria: B.C. Provincial Museum, Special Publication No. 2, 1947.

PETERS, H. S. *and* BURLEIGH, T. D., *The Birds of Newfoundland*. St. John's: Newfoundland Department of Natural Resources, 1951.

SALT, W. RAY, *and* WILK, A. L., *The Birds of Alberta*. Edmonton: Alberta Department of Economic Affairs, 1958.

SNYDER, L. L., *Ontario Birds*. Toronto: Clarke, Irwin, 1950.

SQUIRES, W. AUSTIN, *The Birds of New Brunswick*. Saint John: The New Brunswick Museum (Monographic Series No. 4), 1952.

TAVERNER, P. A., *Birds of Canada*. Ottawa: Canadian Department of Mines Bulletin No. 72, 1934.

TUFTS, ROBIE W., *The Birds of Nova Scotia*. Halifax: Nova Scotia Museum, 1961.

Periodicals

There are many publications produced regularly by local, provincial and other bird clubs and organizations. The following brief selection is considered fundamental for the birdwatcher in this region:

AMERICAN ORNITHOLOGISTS' UNION, *The Auk*.

CANADIAN AUDUBON SOCIETY, *Canadian Audubon*.

FEDERATION OF ONTARIO NATURALISTS, *The Ontario Naturalist*.

NATIONAL AUDUBON SOCIETY, *Audubon*.

SASKATCHEWAN NATURAL HISTORY SOCIETY, *The Blue Jay*.

WILSON ORNITHOLOGICAL SOCIETY, *The Wilson Bulletin*.

Index

On the Making of this Book

The type chosen is Palatino,
a design created by Hermann Zapf for
Stempel Linotype, Frankfurt, and first issued in 1950.
It is a Roman face with broad letters and strong, inclined serifs
resembling the Venetian. Named after the sixteenth-century Italian
writing master Palatino, this type is highly legible and
has retained the aesthetic sculptural
form of the Venetian letter.

Type was set in Canada by Howarth & Smith Monotype, Limited, Toronto

Printed and bound in England by
Balding + Mansell Limited, Wisbech and London

The drawings on pages preceding the plates were reproduced
from J. Fenwick Lansdowne's preliminary sketches.